MUSIC
IN YOUR
CHURCH

MUSIC
IN YOUR
WILLIAM C. HUNTER
CHURCH

**A Guide for Pastors,
Music Committees,
and Music Leaders**

Judson Press® Valley Forge

MUSIC IN YOUR CHURCH

Copyright © 1981
Judson Press, Valley Forge, PA 19481

Library of Congress Cataloging in Publication Data

Hunter, William C.
    Music in your church.

    1. Music in churches. 2. Church music. I. Title.
ML3001.H88   783'.02'6   81-4933
ISBN 0-8170-0917-5   AACR2

The name JUDSON PRESS is registered as a trademark in the U.S. Patent Office.
Printed in the U.S.A. ⊕

Contents

The Magic of Music

There is a sort of magic to music. Henry Tuckerman, an American author of the 1800s, said this: "Explain it as we may, a martial strain will urge a man into the front rank of battle sooner than an argument, and a fine anthem will excite his devotion more certainly than a logical discourse." An educator said to me one time, "I do not mean to belittle your sermons, but an invitation hymn does more to reach me than even a good sermon." I hope that this would not be true of everyone, because the mind must be reached as well as the emotions. But we are only being realistic when we recognize that music of the right kind does lend itself to the language of faith. Music reaches our aesthetic nature and our emotions. Music says something that the spoken word is powerless to say. Church music is a powerful ally of the Word of God. A church without music is like a body without breath.

Even those who cannot play an instrument, or even carry a tune, can and do enjoy good music—and usually love to sing! I doubt that any investigation could establish the following opinion, but it is something of a conviction: The quality of church music reflects the quality of church character. This needs to be explained. By "quality of church music" I refer to the total range of church musical experience: congregational singing, solo and small group performance, the choir, and instrumentalists. Excellence is not only measured by technical excellence in the rendition of music, but also by the enthusiasm and wholeheartedness with which the church engages in singing, as well as that with which it provides for its choir, its director, and its instrumentalists. Even in small churches with small resources, the vitality of church life is reflected by the church's music.

A minister works hard to prepare a good sermon and a board of trustees provides for the cleanliness and maintenance of the church building; so must the entire church body do everything possible to provide for good music and good singing in the church. It is a matter of vital importance.

1
The Pastor's Responsibility for Church Music

The thousands who sing together at a Billy Graham evangelistic rally sing with a fervor that is contagious. One doesn't feel depressed or full of doubts while all around people are singing, "To God be the glory! Great things He hath done!" or "Rejoice! the Lord is King." Hymns express faith and also create a mood. When people sing together joyfully, they are united emotionally and spiritually. They are prepared to work together and worship together. The hymn is a valuable channel for expressing faith and developing faith.

The member of a small church sometimes suffers from feelings of frustration in congregational singing. He or she attends a huge rally of Christians, where voices are joined in a surge of joyful power. Trained leaders direct the singing, and capable organists or pianists accompany the singing. This individual returns to his or her own little church where the hymn singing is a letdown. In this congregation, too many voices seem raspy, and some voices are not in tune. The tempo drags and the people sing with an effort. It comes as something of a relief when the hymn is finally concluded! Fortunately, this is not the experience of *all* small churches.

Pastors and music directors have frustrations of their own. The pastor may have chosen a hymn of profound significance, one that reinforces the major points of the sermon. But if it is a hymn with which the congregation is unacquainted, they stumble over it or sing it less than halfheartedly. Someone is sure to grumble, "Why doesn't the pastor stick to the 'old favorites'?" If the church is fortunate enough to have a music director with professional training, it may have another problem. The director may wish to lead the congregation in singing the nobler hymns—hymns with dignity, beauty, and profound theological meaning. But to the director's dismay, he or she may find people resisting these efforts and calling for songs with bouncy, swingy, rollicking tunes and shallow sentiments.

Your church is fortunate if it has none of these problems, or if it has them only rarely. They are rather common problems, however, especially in small or medium-sized churches. If you have an abundance of trained vocal talent, or even untrained natural talent, your church will have these problems less than others. But you may not have an abundance of trained or natural talent, and in this chapter I would like to show how the pastor can contribute to good church music.

Sensing the Worship Needs of the Congregation

The pastor really has two roles: (1) as *leader,* to provide what he or she believes to be best for the congregation, and (2) as *servant,* to furnish what the congregation interprets to be its needs. Hymns are a vital part of the church's worship experience, but people's hymn preferences are as varied as the people themselves. A paraphrase of Abraham Lincoln's words is appropriate: "You can please all of the people some of the time; you can please some of the people all of the time; but you cannot please all of the people all of the time." The person who complains, "Why don't they ever sing our favorite hymns?" *really* means, "Why don't they sing *my* favorite song more often?"

There is no magic solution for pleasing everyone's tastes in Christian music, but perhaps we need to try a little more diligently than we have been. A truly Christian person should develop a breadth of appreciation for the great variety of Christian music forms. Walls of partition between different styles of music have broken down somewhat within our churches during the past decade. In some churches, those walls could afford to tumble down even more.

Here is what I mean: Those who admire the classic hymns of dignity, depth, and majesty should also be open to the gospel song and even the occasional chorus. Those who are fond of the chorus and the gospel song should be eager to include more of the classic hymns in their repertoire. The exponent of the classic hymns should recognize that others in the church do have valid and valuable worship experiences related to choruses and gospel songs. This person should relax and try to share in the worshipful use of these songs.

Beyond question, church congregations represent a wide diversity of worship styles, from free style to formal. The particular style of one congregation at a given time may change perceptibly with a change of pastors. Congregations *do* change. It seems logical to assume that there is enough diversity within most congregations to accommodate the coexistence of different types of songs and hymns. A synthesis of these styles would not compromise the integrity of the worship but would enrich it.

I believe, though, that congregations should be educated to the essential differences in worship songs. We should be aware of the fact that the simple tunes and the catch choruses become popular because of their rhythm. They are no substitute for the hymns that express profound faith in beautiful musical and poetic form. Hymns of majesty and dignity should never be excluded from worship, even by congregations that have a shortage of vocal talent.

How does a pastor provide for variety in music tastes when he or she has only one hymnal? This will be discussed in the chapter on the music committee, under the subject "The Selection of Hymnals."

Samples of Hymns, Gospel Songs, and Choruses

Strictly speaking, the word "hymn" probably includes what we have come to call a "gospel song," as well as songs of sublime dignity. Not every hymn, however, is a "gospel song." My efforts to define "gospel song" will probably flounder, since gospel songs do not uniformly and precisely fit one definition. Generally speaking, though, gospel songs use either catchy rhythms or dotted note patterns to achieve a singable effect. The gospel song tends to deal with conversion, the atonement, or heaven more than with other themes. Some songs blend characteristics of both hymns and gospel songs. They are difficult to classify.

There are some gospel songs that are so "swingy" in character that one could very easily dance or roller skate to them. Further pursuit of this matter could lead me into the deep waters of controversy, and there I do not wish to go! But perhaps the church *has* been too stiff and somber; perhaps it needs a little liveliness. In earlier reference to this question, I advocated balanced use of hymns of dignity, gospel songs, and choruses. Each individual needs to do some intensive thinking about the question "What is real worship?"

Choruses are usually very catchy, recurrent in their phraseology, and quite simple in the thought they express. If the words alone were recited, they would not be considered profound sentiment or beautiful poetry.

It would be useful and illustrative to give samples of what we define as "hymns," "gospel songs," and "choruses."

Hymns

"A Mighty Fortress Is Our God"

"The Church's One Foundation"

"O God Our Help in Ages Past"

"Jesus, the Very Thought of Thee"

"Rejoice, the Lord Is King"

"Ye Servants of God, Your Master Proclaim"

"Guide Me, O Thou Great Jehovah"

"Holy, Holy, Holy"

"Love Divine, All Loves Excelling"

"My Faith Looks Up to Thee"

"Fairest Lord Jesus"

Gospel Songs

"In the Garden"

"The Old Rugged Cross"

"Blessed Assurance"

"Praise Him! Praise Him!"

"More About Jesus"

"What a Friend We Have in Jesus"

"Since Jesus Came into My Heart"

"I Know Whom I Have Believed"

"Savior, Like a Shepherd Lead Us"

"Tell Me the Stories of Jesus"

"When the Roll Is Called Up Yonder"

Choruses

"His Name Is Wonderful"

"Surely Goodness and Mercy"

"Christ for Me"

"He Lives"

"Pass It On"

"If You Want Joy"

"They'll Know We Are Christians by Our Love"

"Happiness Is the Lord"

"Just a Closer Walk with Thee"

"He's Everything to Me"

"Lonesome Valley"

"He's Got the Whole World in His Hands"

It seems reasonable to expect that:

- every Christian develop an appreciation for the best in hymnology.
- gospel songs be included in the format of worship.
- some worship occasions be provided for those who enjoy choruses.
- Christians be cognizant of the wide variety of worship "tastes" and not be contemptuous or impatient with those whose tastes differ from their own.

Familiar Tunes for Unfamiliar Hymns

When the pastor finds a hymn that is especially appropriate to the sermon topic, he or she may reduce the usual resistance to a new hymn by having the congregation sing it to a familiar tune. This is not as difficult as it sounds. In some hymnals, hymns are not only listed by title and opening verse, but also by *meter*. Here is how to take an unfamiliar hymn and sing it to a familiar tune: (1) Note the meter of the tune (written under the hymn title); (2) Turn back to the metrical index, find that meter, and note the various hymns written to it; (3) Refer to the hymns listed until you find one you feel is fairly familiar to your congregation; (4) Give your organist the page of the hymn whose *tune* you are singing. In the bulletin give the hymn title, the page number of the *words* you are singing and a note in parentheses saying, "sung to the tune of _____."

Usually this substitution of a familiar tune for an unfamiliar one will work well, but occasionally one will encounter a little awkwardness in fitting the words of the original tune to the substitute tune. It would be good to have the choir sing through the hymn on rehearsal night, so that if any serious difficulty should surface, that hymn could be completely replaced by another one before Sunday morning worship.

Illustration of Singing an Unfamiliar Hymn to a Familiar Tune

(unfamiliar) Hymn No. 602 "Thou Gracious God Whose
Mercy Lends"
Angelus L.M.
(tune name and meter)

Comment: *L.M.* is a rhythm pattern to which the tune "Angelus" conforms. We look in the back of the hymnal and find that sixty-nine other hymns have been written to that same meter. In other words, we can exchange our unfamiliar tune for one of those many other tunes, provided our congregation is familiar with the one we substitute.

(familiar) Hymn No. 527 "Jesus Shall Reign Where'er the
Sun"
Duke Street L.M.
(tune name and meter)

This would appear in the bulletin as follows:

Hymn No. 602 "Thou Gracious God Whose Mercy Lends" (sung to the tune of "Jesus Shall Reign")

Don't give the page number of "Jesus Shall Reign" in the bulletin. That would merely confuse the congregation. Be content with the bare statement that this song is being sung to the tune of "Jesus Shall Reign."

Prepare the Organist and Choir Director

The organist especially must be given the page number of "Jesus Shall Reign" in order to be familiar with it and have it ready to play when the unfamiliar hymn has been announced. If the choir director and choir have had even a brief opportunity to rehearse the hymn to the more familiar tune, they will give better leadership and be more composed. The pastor and the entire church would benefit if the choir were given Sunday's hymns on their rehearsal before that Sunday. The choir members give tremendous leadership in congregational singing when they are familiar with the hymns being sung.

Group Solidarity

Experience proves that people who are in proximity to one another feel more confident to sing out. They are more conscious of their effort being a group effort. Yet on their own people do not sit in neat, well-packed rows. They scatter. Times without number I have announced, "As we sing this next hymn, please move so that everyone is sitting in the six (or whatever) rows on this side." Obediently they move, and the singing is infinitely improved. Fortunate are those pastors whose morning and evening congregations are so large that the people must sit close together if they would find a seat!

This reshuffling of seating can be avoided if the rear pew seats are cordoned off with a fabric or metal chain that can be stretched across the pew entrance and snapped onto a hook. There will be a more natural concentration of people closer to the front. They will sing so much better!

Featuring a Hymn

Occasionally the pastor can introduce a worthy hymn to the congregation by making it the feature hymn of the month. When an unfamilar hymn is used on any given Sunday, be sure familiar hymns are included in the worship schedule. Use the feature hymn each Sunday for a month. Once or twice during the month, tell something interesting about that hymn. Have the choir sing it while the congregation listens and follows the words in the hymnal. Have the organist play it for a prelude, an offertory, or a postlude. Read the words without the music, so the congregation can concentrate on the hymn's message. Featuring a hymn will enhance the hymn and help members to add it to their repertoire as one of their favorites.

Should a Pastor Sing in the Choir?

Somehow, through eight years of a pastorate, I managed to avoid any participation in the choir. After all, I argued, there are too few nights free for calling in homes when the husband is there; so why use up one of those few precious free nights singing in the choir? Besides, aren't choirs noted for little jealousies and hurt feelings over who gets to sing and who doesn't? Wouldn't a pastor be wise to avoid any entangling alliances with his church choir? Don't pastors have enough trouble without borrowing any more?

One evening, during choir rehearsal time, I paused to exchange pleasantries with the choir. The members seized the occasion to recruit me for the bass section "just to help out with the cantata." In that moment of weakness, I yielded— and found myself singing with the choir for the next fifteen years! I look back upon those years of choir fellowship with a warm feeling, and with the feeling that the choir has been a fertile field of pastoral ministry.

Since every pastor is different, each one will discover an area where he or she functions best. Some will develop creative rapport with church boards, some with prayer groups, and some with formal counseling sessions. Obviously, every minister should find his or her own niche and work where he or she fits best. There is no clear-cut bit of wisdom indicating that *every* minister should sing in the choir, but likewise, there should be no foregone conclusion that ministers should not sing in the choir. Most ministers seem to have reasonably fair singing voices, but undoubtedly there are ministers who cannot carry a tune! The minister's own talent—or lack of it—should exercise considerable influence over the decision to sing or not to sing in the church's choir.

For me, singing in my choir has created comradeship and rapport with the choir people that has opened doors of service and enhanced my ministry to the choir people and their families. There are not many other groups in the church that meet as frequently and as regularly as the choir meets and that work together as diligently as the choir works. A pastor who can sing, and who has the humility to take a back seat, may be in for a pleasant surprise with the discovery that the choir is a good place to get to know his or her people better and win their confidence.

Summary of Suggestions for Pastors

1. Provide a balanced variety of hymns for congregational worship.

2. Try substituting a familiar tune to an unfamiliar hymn.

3. Furnish Sunday's hymns in advance for the choir to sing at its rehearsal time.

4. Gather the congregation closer together for a feeling of solidarity in singing.

5. Feature a hymn for a period of several Sundays.

6. Go ahead and sing in the choir if your talent enables you to do so.

2
The Music Committee

The music committee occupies a strategic position in the church music program. It has an opportunity to help avoid pitfalls and to plan for maximum enjoyment of church music by everyone.

Selecting the Committee

For a small church, the committee might reasonably consist of six members, plus some ex officio members. For a larger church, the committee could be enlarged by a few more regular members and a few more ex officio members. The ex officio members could include the organist(s) and pianist(s) who regularly perform the service of accompanist for church services. Directors of adult, youth, and children's choirs could be ex officio participants. The pastor and music director (if the church has one) should be invited to every meeting, but other ex officio members need not necessarily be included every time if the agenda does not include items pertaining particularly to them. On some occasions, the regularly appointed/elected members of the committee need to evaluate the various aspects of the music program, and they may feel more freedom to do this if those whom they are evaluating are not present at the meeting.

Two or more members of the committee should be from the adult choir. The others should be faithful members of the congregation known to have level heads and good judgment. If they are also proficient in music, so much the better, but this should not be made a requirement for committee membership.

A good music committee can sift complaints, consider problems, and make recommendations in such a way that the worship program of the church is strengthened and tensions are dissolved.

Terms of Office

Regardless of how the committee is formed—whether it is elected or appointed—there should be rotation of the committee membership. I recommend a two-year term for each member, with rotation each year, so that half the committee would either be elected or appointed every year. Members could be reelected or reappointed, but they should be limited to three consecutive terms (six years) with reelection possible after one year of absence from the committee. Without such a limitation on terms, there might not be enough opportunity for new talent to be added to the committee. From a feeling of obligation, and a fear of hurting someone's feelings, nominating committees often renominate the same people term after term after term.

Responsibilities

The music committee works with the choirs, the directors, the accompanists, and the pastor toward the performance of happy, satisfying Christian music. It seeks to communicate the "grass roots" feelings of the congregation to the leaders in the music program. It listens openly and sympathetically to ideas of the music leaders and tries to serve as a sounding board for those ideas. The committee will seek out, interview, and recommend choir directors, organists, pianists, or music directors when these are needed. It will arrange for tuning and maintenance of organ and pianos. It will mediate complaints concerning music personnel or the music program. It will present a budget for music to the budget committee of the church when the budget is being prepared. It will research and select new hymnals when these are needed.

Occasionally the music committee has the unpleasant task of counseling with personnel who should consider resigning. Sometimes the committee can make some loving, constructive suggestions that will save a music leader from having to resign.

Keeping Records

As with every board and committee of the church, the music committee should keep careful minutes of its meetings. Previous minutes should be read at the beginning of a meeting, and minutes of the current meeting should be read at the close of the meeting to check them for accuracy. Whenever any difficult or touchy subject is discussed, we tend to discuss or debate it, without making any motions or reaching any clear-cut conclusions. A good meeting will give a clear-cut answer to some of these questions:

- What is to be done?
- Who is to do it?
- If money is involved, where will the money come from?
- Have any deadlines been set for the action to begin or for it to conclude?

● How are we going to accomplish our objective?

Often we suffer discord or delay simply because our decisions were neither specific nor on record.

The Budget

There are expenses of the music program that are apt to be overlooked unless the music committee anticipates them and presents them to the church's budget committee. The choir(s) need an appropriation to buy music. Robes should be dry-cleaned during the year. Pianos should be tuned. Community college courses in music leadership are available, and music publishing houses often have one- or two-day institutes with a review of their music for choir directors or choir members. There are courses for music directors at colleges and summer assembly grounds of most denominations. There are publications for music leaders to which the church can subscribe. Unless provision for these things is made in the budget, they are apt to be omitted or neglected.

In churches which are prosperous, the purchase of music for the choir may be no problem. Even in not-so-prosperous churches, the problem may not be acute if the music committee is alert and attentive to the choir's needs. But if the church budget was adopted with little provision for music, and if the church normally operates on a rather tight budget with little surplus, then the choir may find itself locked into rehashing old music or simply singing from the hymnal.

A music committee needs to be alert and needs to consult with the choir director concerning music needs for the coming year. If there is *no* director at the time the budget is being considered (which happens sometimes), the music committee should nevertheless consult with several knowledgeable choir

members and make some request of the budget committee in
the hope that a director may later be secured. Under the best
of circumstances, some member or members of the choir will
be on the budget committee, even though they may be present
as representatives of some board or organization other than
the choir. They could make an appeal for music funds to be
included in the budget in the event that the music committee
had failed to function. But it is really the task of the music
committee to be present or at least to have a written request in
the hands of the budget committee. There are well-meaning
people who sit on budget committees who report having seen
"a whole box full of old music" and who argue that "the choir
should use that before we buy them any new music."

Cantata music books, both for the Easter season and for
Christmas, are expensive. After several years, a cantata can
be repeated, but neither the choir nor the congregation would
be satisfied with continual repetition. Other older music can
occasionally be reused, but without the continual influx of
new music to balance with the old, the music program of the
choir would become stale. Both choir and congregation need
the challenge of new music as well as the familiarity of the old.

Ideas for Those Who Submit the Music Budget to the Church Budgeting Committee

Choir Director Salary(ies)
- Adult Choir Director
- Youth Choir Director
- Children's Choir Director

Accompanists' Salaries
- Organist
- Pianist

- Continuing Education Costs for Choir Director and/or Organist

Purchase of Music for One Year
- Adult Choir
- Youth Choir
- Children's Choir

Maintenance Expenses
- Pianos Tuned
- Organ Tuned or Repaired
- Robes Cleaned
- Repair of Hymnals

Capital Outlays
- Filing Cabinets and Filing Equipment
- Fund for Replacement of Hymnals
- Fund for New Robes

A Five-Year Goal

The music committee needs to combine a good measure of wisdom along with its enthusiasm for the church music program. Unless a church has been previously conditioned to making generous provision for its music program, it could be startled into hostility by the sudden introduction of large budget items for music programming and training. Everything presented in the music committee's budget might be very reasonable; but if the church has been having serious problems just meeting current expenses, it would not look too favorably upon new, heavy items for the music budget.

At the beginning of the year, the music committee should sit down and set some long-range and short-range goals. Perhaps the pianos haven't been tuned for some time; that would be an item for the first year's goal. Perhaps there is no children's choir and the committee would like to work toward that for the second year. A youth choir could be an objective for the third-year goal. Payment of tuition for a training course for the choir director might be a fourth-year goal. New hymnals might be the fifth-year goal. There is cost connected with each of these goals, and the congregation must be educated to the needs for these items. Sudden demands for a big increase in the music budget could, as we have said, have an adverse effect. A gradual approach to a five-year goal would arouse interest and focus the congregation's energy toward working together to accomplish each goal.

Recruiting Musical Leadership

A good music leader is to a church what a superior athlete is to a team. Excellence in music leadership is a fine combination of talent and training. In this area (musical leadership) there is a great demand and, unfortunately, a scarcity of supply. When a church lacks good leadership in this field, it often turns in desperation to almost anyone who can do at least a halfway decent job of playing the organ or the piano, leading the singing, or directing the choir.

Sometimes this desperation uncovers some real talent, hitherto hidden in the congregation. Spurred by the obvious need and the pleas of fellow Christians for help, a truly fine choir director may emerge. With some experience, some help from outside sources, and loving encouragement from within the church, he or she may prove to be the answer to many prayers.

This *sometimes* happens, but not *always*. Sometimes a truly inadequate person is invited to a position of musical leadership, one who isn't gifted with the instinct to recognize just how inadequate he or she is. Rather than hurt this person's feelings, the congregation endures his or her leadership. We need to consider methods of approach which will give people an opportunity to try out for a position but which will not permanently and prematurely establish them in the position.

The two major positions for which a church needs to recruit personnel are the positions of choir director and organist. In some churches, one person fills both of these positions. This lays a heavy burden of double responsibility on the one who fills both positions. Not every organist is capable of directing, and not every director is capable of playing an organ. Some organist/directors do a beautiful job, but music committees should not routinely assume every organist can also direct. Many organists would refuse to accept this double duty.

In the following paragraphs I will discuss ways to go about recruiting musical leadership; the discussion will fall into three main parts—where to look for recruits, the importance of outlining a procedure for selection, and the question of remuneration. Many concerns are the same whether a committee is choosing a choir director or an organist; where there are special considerations for one or the other, I will note them.

Where to Look

Recruiting an organist or choir director begins with knowing where to look. There are certainly many different ways of obtaining musical leadership. During my thirty-three years of pastoral ministry, the five churches I served recruited their choir directors in the following manner: two came from other churches; two were students contacted for us by their institutions' college administrators; one was director of the high school choir; and five came from within the congregations themselves. In a large city with one or more universities in the area, the recruitment of a good organist or choir director is often not difficult. But in small towns with no college or university nearby, recruitment may be a real problem. Even when there is difficulty, the music committee should not be quick to select just anyone who claims to be an organist or choir director. Take time to find leadership that will be right for your church.

If your church is not too far from a university or community college, let your need be known to the music department there. If you are not near a university, an advertisement in the "help wanted" section of the paper might attract a response from an organist or choir director who at the moment is not working in a church. The local high school music department staff would be another possibility; while a member of the staff might not be free, that person might know someone who would be interested. In looking specifically for an organist, one point of contact would be music stores, especially those that sell organs. Store managers are often in touch with organ teachers and capable organists. Organists often belong to "guilds" that meet periodically. Members communicate with one another and often pass on requests from churches that are searching for an organist.

In my last pastorate I was approached several times by young organists I didn't even know who came into the church requesting the privilege of practicing on our pipe organ. From these contacts, we recruited one full-time organist and one substitute organist.

Outlining a Procedure

The music committee should outline a procedure for securing an organist and choir director. The committee should develop a plan to answer these questions (and any others which the members of your committee think are important):

- How can we observe and sample the abilities of this musician prior to making any formal commitment to engage him or her for regular duty?
- Should our formal commitment be for a limited period of time?
- Shall we agree that the full committee shall be present before we take any vote to engage this musician?

Since the pastor is vitally concerned with the smooth and happy flow of the worship, he or she should definitely be included and consulted when a new musician needs to be recruited for the organ or for choir direction. The choir, too, should have an opportunity to see and hear those being considered so that choir members can reflect their feelings to the music committee.

Even when the hiring procedure is explicitly spelled out in the constitution and/or bylaws, there are well-meaning people who short-circuit the proper procedure by taking matters into their own hands. Pastors are guilty of this. Chairpersons of music committees are guilty of this. Choir directors sometimes try to appoint their own successors. This can—and does—cause trouble. When seeking an organist or choir director, it is worthwhile to make this a matter of congregational prayer and private prayer. It would be helpful to have an item in the bulletin asking for prayer and announcing that the matter of finding and hiring an organist or choir director has been placed in the hands of the music committee.

The music committee should set down in writing the qualifications it feels it needs in an organist or choir director. Under "qualifications" the music committee should decide how it will answer these questions (and others if necessary):

- Shall we ask for any references or recommendations from people who might know of this person's ability?
- Is this person a church member? A professing Christian?
- What is his or her background and experience in Christian service?

In choosing a choir director, one of the intangibles to consider relates to the director's ability to work congenially with people and to maintain good rapport with the choir. Some people have excellent musical ability; they may know everything about music but know very little about people. They may have high standards of performance, but produce music from their choirs that is less pleasing and less spirited than leaders with less training could produce. If a director gives references of previous employment, this personality factor might be more easily judged. But if a director has been chosen from within the congregation, a director who is just developing ability, this factor may not be obvious for some time. But, after all, this is a risk we take in securing leadership of any kind—whether we are hiring a pastor or a football coach.

This, however, brings up the problem of how to deal with an applicant of unknown and untested capability. Careful consideration must always be given in these cases, balancing honesty and practicality with kindness and optimism. In one of my pastorates we found ourselves without an organist, and there seemed to be no response to our search for another one. We engaged a young lady who was a talented pianist to play the piano in lieu of the organ. She had never played an organ, but our need for an organist was a challenge to her. She began taking lessons on the organ, and, because of her innate ability, she soon became a very fine organist. When someone of unknown capability, inside or outside of the congregation, responds to your appeal for an organist, ask this person if he or she would be willing to be guest accompanist for the midweek choir rehearsal and for the Sunday morning worship. This should give you a fairly good idea of the person's capability. This procedure can also be adapted to the search for a choir director. You may be very fortunate in having a gifted and dedicated organist or choir director in your congregation. But you may not be so fortunate. Your church may have someone who *thinks* he or she is capable, and who wants the job of organist or choir director, but who is really unable to perform satisfactorily. In such a case, it could be made very clear to anyone interested in applying for the job that the music committee has certain standards and qualifications that must be met, and that until it discovers a musician able to meet those standards, any organist who plays as a substitute or any director who directs as one must be considered only on a Sunday-by-Sunday basis. In most instances, a final judgment on whether to hire an organist or choir director needs to be postponed until his or her ability can be evaluated. There are exceptions to this; I have already mentioned one (the young lady pianist who eventually became a good organist). Another instance, more recently, was of a young woman organ student who played the church organ with considerable timidity. Quick judgment would have pronounced her unfit for the job, but patience and encouragement are being justified; she is noticeably increasing in ability and gaining confidence.

Lastly, the music committee needs to be specific about what will be expected of the persons who will be organist and choir director. Be able to answer the following questions:

- For how many regular services during the week (including

rehearsal) do we expect this person to be present and serving (e.g., evangelistic services, special speakers, Thanksgiving service, Good Friday service, etc.)?

- For how many months of the year do we expect our organist to play?
- What are the usual places during worship when we expect our organist to play: prelude? silent prayer background? prayer response? offertory? postlude? choir accompaniment? accompaniment for solos, duets, trios, instrumentals, etc.?
- Do we expect our choir director to lead congregational singing?

There may very well be some change in expectations of both organist and choir director from time to time, but new recruits to these responsibilities need to be alerted to the range of duties expected of them.

To Pay or Not to Pay?

In smaller churches especially, there are those who maintain that a church member with musical ability and training should donate his or her services without charge, just as every other volunteer worker does. This point of view is often expressed with regard to the organist and choir director. At this point, experience has some wisdom to share. Undoubtedly, there are many fine musicians who willingly donate their services and who are faithful and dependable in their duty. But it is a mistake to make their example a standard to which *all* organists and *all* choir directors must conform to prove their Christian character and Christian spirit.

Those who like to equate the job of organist or choir director with other volunteer jobs in the church are really overlooking something. These jobs demand excellence for performance before the *total church* Sunday after Sunday. They demand punctual, regular attendance at rehearsal in the middle of the week and punctual, regular attendance at morning worship. They demand working with people, leading people, keeping people happy. The latter qualifications may pertain more to the choir director than to the organist, but the organist also is aware of having to work with people as well as with the organ.

The pay for these jobs is not intended to be a measure of their eternal significance. Organist and choir director are not more important in God's kingdom or in Christ's plan than church school teacher, treasurer, deacon, or youth advisor. The pay is only a recognition that unusually heavy demands are being made upon organist and choir director that are not made upon anyone else in the church. How would the church school teacher feel if he or she had to meet with his or her class *every Wednesday* without fail, as well as on Sunday? How would the teacher feel if it were necessary to have the class ready *every Sunday* to stand up before the congregation prepared to answer Bible questions or put on a skit? How would the treasurer feel if he or she had to meet with the trustees *every Wednesday* and then stand up before the congregation *every Sunday* ready with a complete and up-to-date report that every bill had been paid and every receipt or expense had been entered? I have been a pastor long enough to know that very few members have perfect records even in such a simple thing as worship attendance, and very few members would welcome having to perform acceptably every Sunday under public scrutiny. The organist and choir director deserve the rather modest pay they receive for services performed under strenuous and demanding conditions. If these musicians desire to return their pay as a donation to the church, that is their privilege. Many do just that. But this should be their option. Giving of anything—time or money—should be voluntary, not coerced.

Unquestionably there are times when the music committee will have to look outside the congregation for a trained musician. We cannot demand of some "outsider" that he or she donate his or her services for the sheer joy of getting to serve us. If the church is to have the option of securing an outside musician, there must be provision for remuneration in the budget.

The music committee needs to know in any case what has been provided in the budget for organist and choir director and what previous musicians were paid. If there has been a lapse of time since the church last had an organist or choir director, there may need to be a review of the amount that was paid and a reconsideration of what *should* be paid. Perhaps the previous pay was very low simply because some person without professional training took the job on just a temporary basis. Reconsideration of the pay, and, in fact, of all matters relating to salaries should be referred to the trustees or whoever constitutionally has authority to hire. It is always enlightening to call other churches and learn from them what they pay their organists and their choir directors.

Good Accompaniment

Good accompaniment to congregational singing is especially important to the support of the singing. Do you have a good piano and/or good organ in the sanctuary? Is the piano kept in tune? Are the accompanists given the hymns in advance so that they are familar with them and capable of playing them properly?

An organ, whether pipe organ or electronic organ, is played with a "legato" (sustained) tone. Piano notes are somewhat more "staccato" (sharp and distinct from each other). If an organ alone is the accompaniment to congregational singing, it needs to be played with enough volume to be clearly heard and to provide leadership to the congregation. As with everything, there needs to be moderation here. Some organists, in their eagerness to provide leadership, swell the volume almost to the point of drowning the voices.

If a good piano is also available for hymn accompaniment, the organist need not play so loud. A piano's staccato sound seems to give the congregation a clearer concept of the beat and the precise movement of the hymn. Organ and piano each have a unique contribution to congregational singing, and together they are excellent.

Good Leader

Use your choir director to lead the congregational singing. The choir loft may or may not be the best position from which to direct the congregation. Have the director stand where he or she is visible to all and can be easily followed.

Remember, though, most persons in congregations are notoriously poor at looking up and following a director. They are not trained in reading words, reading notes, and looking up all at the same time. Even if he or she does look up, the average worshiper has little idea of how to correlate the director's motions with the number of beats in a measure or the time value of each note. The director's motions will coordinate the choir and the accompanist(s), and this is very important in keeping correct tempo for a song. If a microphone is nearby, the director can lead with his or her voice as well as by motions of the hands.

Giving Support to a Younger Director

A younger director needs authority to lead older choir members. A certain choir had a college student choir director who was actually very knowledgeable of how music ought to be sung and quick to catch any deviation from correct performance. She had a chalkboard on which she gave short lectures on musical terms and values. She had the choir warm up with the singing of scales and intervals. This was very valuable education. Some choir members who had sung for years confessed to learning things they hadn't known before.

All of this was good, but her method of correcting the erring singer sometimes left him or her smarting with embarrassment. Some of the more experienced singers felt the instruction wasted time which was needed for rehearsal, especially when it covered ground with which they were thoroughly familiar. There were also a few who resented correction from such a young person. The choir lost a few members during this period.

Before hiring a younger director, the music committee should resolve to be supportive of the director and to appeal for patience, understanding, and appreciation from the choir. The committee could suggest changes in the director's techniques when they seem to be meeting with discontent or dissatisfaction. With a little sensible mediation by a caring music committee, the period of leadership by a young director could become a valuable learning exerience for both choir and director.

The Selection of Hymnals

The hymnal is a very important tool of the minister in leading worship; so the music committee should listen very sensitively to his or her expressed needs and wishes in buying new hymnals. Ministers frequently shy away from doing battle for a new hymnal: first, because of the cost of new hymnals; second, because of the trauma of a change. Perhaps some congregations would sooner change ministers than hymnals!

The choice of a new hymnal should be influenced by some objective guidelines and careful procedures. The music committee should do the research and make the decision, under these conditions:

1. The committee should invite the pastor, the choir director, the organist, the pianist, and a few other members of known musical ability to join in the research.

2. The committee should establish these guidelines for selection of a new hymnal:

    a. Clear, reasonably large print of words and music.

    b. Good balance between classic hymns and gospel songs (and perhaps some choruses!).

    c. Mixture of some contemporary Christian songs with the older, established songs. There should be room for growth. Choice should not be limited to mere maintenance of the status quo.

    d. Broad variety of topics (e.g., doctrinal, devotional, practical, missionary, special days, etc.).

    e. Broad choice of responsive readings.

    f. A few extras, such as solos, calls to worship, prayer responses, etc.

3. The committee should take a survey of the congregation's hymn choices. Ask each person to list ten hymns he or she believes ought to be included in a hymnal. Tabulate this survey. Note which hymns gather the most votes. Consider the results to be guiding, but not rigidly binding. Experience

with this type of survey proves that the majority of choices will cluster around hymns and gospel songs of proven value. Examine the hymnals you are seriously considering to see if they contain most of your congregation's favorites. When the committee has tentatively agreed on its choice of a hymnal, it can purchase several copies of the chosen hymnal.

4. The committee can place these few favored hymnals on a table near the back of the sanctuary for members of the congregation to peruse. The committee's choice will be reinforced if members can say honestly, "We had the congregation's preferences in mind when we made our selection."

Congregations which desire frequent use of choruses can print or mimeograph these in little booklets. These will be thin enough to slip into the racks with a hymnal. The choruses usually are taken from some published book of choruses which is kept at the piano for congregational accompaniment. Permission to do this would first have to be secured from the publisher; without this permission, you would be infringing on the copyright. A better alternative would be to buy enough thin chorus booklets to place in the racks with the hymnals. A third alternative is to buy a hymnal which contains a good balance of classic hymns, gospel songs, and choruses.

Summary of Suggestions for the Music Committee

1. Take care in the selection of persons to serve on this committee.

2. Make sure that there is rotation of membership.

3. Keep accurate records.

4. Stay abreast of current needs when preparing the budget; plan for the long-range future.

5. Plan carefully in recruiting musical leadership.

6. Be sure to support a younger director in his or her position.

7. Take into consideration the needs and tastes of the congregation when choosing a hymnal.

3
The Responsibilities of the Choir Director

The choir director is the leader of the choir and often is the director of the music program in the church. As leader of the choir he or she is responsible for seeing that the choir fulfills its purpose in the church. The responsibilities of the choir director include: scheduling of choir music, auditioning new choir members, leading rehearsals, planning for and implementing any choir participation in special church occasions, bringing the choir back together after summer vacation, giving attention to details—such as processionals and proper amplification of sound—and organizing special singing occasions (i.e., an evening hymn sing).

Scheduling of Choir Music

Scheduling of choir music is the prerogative of the choir director. He or she should sit down with the pastor and the church calendar and note what themes will be appropriate for particular Sundays. This is not very difficult. Holy days and national holidays usually inspire musicians to write music for these occasions. The director can go through the file of music on hand or else order music in advance.

The real challenge is to be prepared with music on the theme of the pastor's sermon. If the pastor is a well-organized person, he or she may be able to furnish the director with themes and Scriptures to be used for the next twelve months and the exact date on which each sermon will be preached. Sometimes the pastor is unable to do this. When preaching expository sermons on a book of the Bible, the pastor may not really know how big a "chunk" to bite off for each sermon until he or she has done the hard work of actually preparing the sermon. On some occasions, the pastor will be preaching topical sermons, and these can be better predicted in advance.

Choir directors usually appreciate it when a pastor gives them sermon themes or topics in advance. This gives meaning and purpose to their work. They like to support and reinforce the pastor in the work of communicating a message. Choir members also are more cooperative when they understand that music is not just chosen at random or just because the director happens to like the sound of a particular piece of music.

Auditioning Prospective Choir Members

Recruitment of capable voices for the choir is undoubtedly the stiffest challenge facing a good director. Most church choirs are continually in need of more good voices in all sections. At the risk of severe oversimplification we can list the volunteer choir voices in one of three categories: (1) good voices with some ability to read notes; (2) good voices with little ability to read notes; (3) mediocre—or worse—voices with little ability to read notes.

When I use the phrase "ability to read notes," I imply ability to sing a part as written. Strangely enough, some people are endowed with a voice of very pleasant tone quality but they cannot carry a tune unless surrounded by strong voices that do not waver from the right notes.

To the three categories above, there might be added two more: (4) people who instinctively "home in" on the melody even though they are assigned a harmony part and (5) people who are incapable of singing anything but discord, no matter *how* well flanked with good voices.

In every choir there are some well-intentioned people who feel compelled to issue a general invitation to "one and all" to "come join the choir!" This broad invitation they make even broader by adding, "You don't need to know how to sing. Just come and make a joyful noise to the Lord like the rest of us." It is hoped that someone with good sense would warn the "monotone" what a disaster his or her voice would be in a small choir, so that the director might be spared the frustration of having to encounter that voice in his choir.

Some church choirs have the stipulation that anyone interested in joining the choir should first talk to the director. The director can casually and pleasantly talk about the choir with the applicant and can ask him or her to sing a few notes with the piano to help the director to get the range of his or her voice and so to learn in which section he or she should be placed. If this little audition discloses a voice of rather hopeless quality, the director can gently suggest to the applicant that there might be a job in the church for which he or she is better suited.

Of course the choir people themselves set the tone for recruitment. If they have a low opinion of themselves and are indifferent about whether their performance is shabby or good, they will recruit without discernment or any concern for the consequences. If, however, the choir has some respect for what it does, and concern for how it is done, recruitment will be tempered with a little caution and good sense.

Recruitment is also conditioned by the size of the church and the number of talented people available to sing. Obviously, a small church cannot be as selective as a large church. But having acknowledged that, I still feel that even a small choir in a small church can have pride in what it does. Numbers alone do not improve a choir's performance. A small choir of disciplined singers, conscientiously responsive to the director's leadership, can produce worshipful, meaningful song.

In nearly every church there are a few persons in each choir section whose voices are true to pitch and who can read notes. They can be centrally seated in their section to help those who do not read notes but who can listen and follow. "Reading notes" is a skill that can be acquired by patient experience. Quality of choir performance will improve as members with no training are faithful in learning.

A System for Rehearsals

We have discussed previously the value of planning ahead for music that correlates with the pastor's sermons and special occasions of the church calendar year. Obviously, this is the first necessary step toward a systematic rehearsal system. But this is not the entire answer. Knowing in advance what music is to be sung is of slight value unless the director has a good system for advance preparation of the music.

If the inventory of music on file is low, then of course the director's choices will be severely limited. Older music can be sung again, but there probably should be a substantial lapse of time before the music is repeated. There should be a balanced diet of newer music with the older music. Advance scheduling of music and an adequate rehearsal system are closely tied in with the adequate supply of music.

Suppose the supply of music *is* adequate. Suppose the director has been able to schedule in advance his or her dates for singing each piece of music. What system will the director use to prepare that music?

How does it work when a choir comes to rehearsal with no previous contact with a piece of music and must have that piece ready for delivery the next Sunday? Most likely, the entire evening of rehearsal would need to be devoted to that piece. If the choir consists of trained, talented singers, this would probably be no problem. In reality, however, most of our choirs are not so fortunate as to be composed entirely, or even in majority, of trained and talented voices. What usually happens when a choir prepares a piece with only one rehearsal is that human memory doesn't retain every detail of the rehearsal. The choir always feels a little bit of nervous panic on Sunday morning when it rises to sing, and then only the things that have been diligently drilled into it by repetition really stay with it. Without the background of several rehearsals on a piece, some bass will surely come booming in when the women only are supposed to sing. Some sopranos will throw the choir into temporary confusion by jumping the gun on a rest. Or several members who were not at rehearsal robe up with the choir and sing anyhow on Sunday, in the hope that a miracle will take place and they will sing as well as if they had been to rehearsal.

Directors who plan ahead are able to expose the choir to several different anthems on a given evening of rehearsal.

There are several advantages to this. One is to give a little variety to rehearsal night. Intensive drilling on just one piece of music, under pressure to have it ready for Sunday, can be a bit tedious and monotonous. Another advantage is that it gives the director the feel of the music—some idea of where there may be difficulty and how to direct the music most effectively. Most important is the value to the choir of the repeated impact of the music, stretched over a period of several weeks. First exposure to a piece may be quite short; the choir may only read through it. Each rehearsal thereafter, a little more time and effort is concentrated on that piece until the final rehearsal when it is polished for performance. During the preceding weeks, the memory has had a chance to store its experience with that piece. Every rehearsal awakens that memory, refreshes it, and establishes it. It is not the best policy for a choir member to sing on Sunday if he or she has missed the last rehearsal, but if it seems necessary to use every choir member present in order to "field a full team," those who missed last week's rehearsal have a fair chance of singing the music correctly if they were exposed to it over several previous rehearsals.

A good director will always be introducing some new pieces and also returning to older pieces for confirmation of what has been learned and for further development of confidence in the choir members and their knowledge of the music.

Sample of a Continuing Schedule for Choir Rehearsals

The following schedule should be considered a flexible pattern for rehearsals, rather than something rigid. Some pieces are more difficult than others and so would require a disproportionate amount of time for rehearsal. This, however, is an illustration of how a rehearsal system should weave together preparation for performances far-off and performance next Sunday, with the balance of rehearsal time weighted in favor of the impending performance.

January

Week 1—Cantata for Easter (fifteen minutes of rehearsal time)
For next Sunday—Piece "A" (thirty minutes of rehearsal time)
For two Sundays away—Piece "B" (twenty-five minutes of rehearsal time)
For three Sundays away—Piece "C" (twenty minutes of rehearsal time)
TOTAL TIME—ONE AND ONE-HALF HOURS (same for each rehearsal)

Week 2—Cantata (fifteen minutes)
For next Sunday—Piece "B" (thirty minutes)
For two Sundays away—Piece "C" (twenty-five minutes)
For three Sundays away—Piece "D" (twenty minutes)

Week 3, etc.—Continue the pattern of thirty minutes for next Sunday's anthem, twenty-five minutes for the anthem two Sundays away, twenty minutes for the piece three Sundays away, and always fifteen minutes on the Easter cantata.

Two Months Before the Cantata

Every week—Cantata (twenty-five minutes)

>For next Sunday (thirty minutes)
>For two Sundays away (twenty minutes)
>For three Sundays away (fifteen minutes)

One Month Before the Cantata
Every week—Cantata (forty minutes)
>For next Sunday (thirty minutes)
>For two Sundays away (fifteen minutes)
>For three Sundays away (five minutes)

The Week Before the Cantata
Schedule an extra night, or a Saturday or Sunday afternoon, for sole attention to cantata rehearsal.

Length of Time for a Rehearsal

Some choirs have only one hour for rehearsal. Some have two hours. It seems to me that one hour is really not enough, but two hours *every* rehearsal night for people who have worked all day long gets to be a bit wearisome. If choir members will only show up on time and have a prompt beginning, an hour and a half provides a very substantial length of time for rehearsal.

The few minutes of rehearsal just before the choir emerges from the robing room on Sunday morning are extremely important in reminding the choir of all they have learned in the past few weeks. It will equip the choir with an extra feeling of confidence and poise that makes for better performance.

The Use of Choir Folders

If the choir has a good rehearsal system, it will practice not just one, but several pieces of music during a rehearsal session. This could mean considerable time consumed just handing out music and then collecting it again. This is not necessary. Each choir member should have a folder which has four to six elastic strings inside the cover at the fold. Also inside such a folder, on each cover, are flaps or pockets capable of holding music. In this way each choir member has and becomes acquainted with the music that is being prepared for immediate use and future use. The director can advise the choir to mark lightly in pencil, on the cover of the music, the prospective date for the use of each piece of music. This helps each person to realize there is continuity and correlation to what the choir is doing. For Sunday service, the folders have a little more dignity than loose pieces of music. Every folder should have its owner's name on the inside of the cover on marking tape.

The Choir and Special Occasions

Holy Week and Christmas are peak seasons of devotion and enthusiasm in our Christian faith. Anticipation builds toward these events. People are willing to exert extra effort and extra energy in preparing suitable music for Easter and Christmas. Since cantatas or equivalent music programs usually require about three months of advance preparation, the total result of preparation for Easter and Christmas is six months of extra incentive and extra stimulation for choir endeavor. Interest, enthusiasm, and a sense of purpose are very important to good performance.

Cantatas

A cantata is valuable to the choir and to the church because of the music's spiritual impact. A cantata frequently attracts new choir members who agree to enroll in the choir for a limited period of cantata preparation and delivery. Quite often, however, some of these people find the choir so enjoyable that they become permanent members.

A cantata requires continuous, concentrated effort. Most cantatas cover the wide range of redemption's story, and they challenge the choir to its best performance. In other words, the cantata creates a long-range motivation for the choir's efforts.

Interest and incentive can be further enhanced by arranging a guest performance of your cantata for some other church. There are many small churches which have no choir. They welcome an offer from some other church to present an Easter or Christmas cantata to them. Perhaps we can understand why they appreciate an offer like this when we reflect on the cost and effort of arranging for a choir under other conditions. Traveling choirs usually ask for a meal, overnight lodging, and a generous offering. This is fine and usually quite rewarding. But a small church may be reluctant to involve itself in such a big effort very often. Some churches are loath to assume such heavy responsibility; when a church from their own town or a neighboring town offers to come sing, with no preconditions or financial demands, they are delighted. Sometimes the host church will voluntarily take an offering for the visiting choir, which can be used to buy music, but this should not be expected or required.

Usually arrangements for a visiting performance are made by the choir's pastor. He or she can suggest that the hosts arrange for a coffee hour afterward, with light refreshments, so the hosts and their visitors can fellowship after the cantata.

This guest performance of the cantata is reciprocal in value. It is a treat for the host church and a blessing to the guest choir to know it can perform a useful service to others. There is another fringe benefit to the guest choir: The guest performance is usually prior to the performance in the choir's home church, so that the guest performance becomes a full-force rehearsal.

As I diagrammed in my rehearsal schedule earlier, a little of the cantata can be practiced at each choir rehearsal, thus allowing the choir also to work on its regular Sunday-by-Sunday schedule of music.

Additional Occasions

It is not always possible to anticipate a year in advance every occasion on which one would need the choir to sing. Some occasions to keep in mind would be these: Maundy Thursday, Good Friday, a Union Thanksgiving Service, a candlelight Christmas Eve service, when the local church is host to a convention or conference, and ecumenical events, such as World Day of Prayer.

Sample of a Church Music Calendar for One Year

To this calendar should be added the rehearsal times of the choir or choirs and the scheduled meetings of the music committee.

January 1 to Easter—The adult choir begins preparation of its Easter cantata, along with rehearsals of its regular Sunday worship anthems.

March—Church hosts some visiting musical group, e.g., Christian college choir, band, quartet, noted instrumentalist or soloist, etc.

Palm Sunday—Choir gives its cantata for a neighboring church or a church in a nearby city.

Maundy Thursday or Good Friday—Choir offers one or more pieces for these Holy Week services.

Easter—Sunday morning or Sunday evening: Easter cantata.

May—Music festival. Potluck dinner in evening. Performance following with use of nearly all of the church's music resources: adult choir, youth choir, children's choir, vocal groups, instrumentalists, soloists, organ, piano, *and* congregational singing.

   —Mother's Day: Youth choir sings.

June—Children's Day or Father's Day: Children's choir sings.

September 1 to Christmas—Choirs begin preparation of cantatas, along with regular music.

September—Director of adult choir begins prerehearsal instruction series on the basics of music.

November—Thanksgiving music. Choir may have part in Union Thanksgiving Service. Special music also for choir's own church.

December—Sunday before Christmas Sunday:

- *Morning,* Youth and children's choirs sing special Christmas music.
- *Evening,* Adult choir presents the Christmas cantata.
- *Christmas Eve,* Candlelight service; choir sings one or more pieces.

Resuming Choir After a Summer Vacation

After a summer vacation many choir members will be eager to resume regular rehearsals and Sunday performance. But even this eagerness is mixed with some inertia that must be overcome. One must forsake the luxury of relaxing after dinner is over and the dishes are done. Darkness begins to settle earlier, and it seems to take a little more effort to launch out into the darkness after a full day of work. The recliner, the television, and the crackling fireplace are quite inviting. The habit of regular midweek choir rehearsal has been broken and that habit must be reestablished. Resumption of rehearsals should be in the bulletin at least two weeks in advance. The Sunday before the actual resumption of rehearsals, the printed announcement should be given a little boost by a verbal announcement by the pastor or perhaps by the choir director. That same afternoon a letter to each choir member could be dropped in the mail as a follow-up of Sunday's announcement. Following is a suggested letter:

Dear Choir Member,

I hope you have had a good summer and are rested and ready to resume singing in First Baptist Church Choir. We have some excellent music picked out for worship enjoyment. It is a pleasure and a privilege to sing for the glory of God. We receive far more than we give. In our choir, everyone is important. We need everyone, and we want everyone. We are counting on you. Let nothing prevent you from being with us at rehearsal this Wednesday evening at 7:30 P.M. at the church. Following our rehearsal, we will have a coffee time with light refreshments in the social hall. We'll see you there.

Cordially yours,

_____(signed by the choir director, chairman of the music committee, or some member of the choir)

Here is a suggested bulletin announcement for fall resumption of choir rehearsals:

Positions Open: In soprano, alto, tenor, and bass sections of our choir.

Physical Qualifications: You must be able to carry a melody or harmony part and have vision good enough to see the choir director ten feet away.

Experience: No applications will be accepted from persons who have not sung, whistled, or hummed a tune at work, in the bathtub or shower, or at some time in their lives.

Beginning Wage: Guaranteed satisfaction and joy in the service of the Lord and the church.

Fringe Benefits—Social Security: We can assure the security of social fellowship with other choir members.

To Apply: New help should talk to our director, (*director's name*), as soon as possible.

Rehearsals Start: September ____, 7:30 P.M. in the sanctuary.

Processionals

Choir processionals can be somewhat rugged and unimpressive without sufficient preparation before Sunday. A processional really needs to be practiced during rehearsal. If choristers are to enter the sanctuary two-by-two, be sure they are correctly matched up before entry. Rehearse the art of keeping step together, and of keeping the tempo so that the choir members entering at the rear of the sanctuary aren't a half beat behind the choir members at the front of the sanctuary. Be sure each one knows where he or she is to sit and is in the correct position in the line so that the seating arrangement will fall in place naturally.

Microphones

Proper amplification of the choir is an art and a science. Some professional help should be secured to arrange microphones and amplifiers. Some choirs may not feel they need or can afford electronic assistance. However, when a soloist is involved, a microphone is really an essential requirement for good balance with the choir. Since few church choir soloists have concert hall quality voices, their solo performance can be improved by microphone assistance. Their words will be much more audible and the sound of their voices will be enhanced.

An Evening Hymn Sing

The choir director, or a committee appointed by the director, could plan an evening hymn sing with extra features. Purchase one or more books that tell how hymns came to be written. Tell a particular story and tell something about the author. Alternate congregational singing with numbers by the choir, solos, duets, trios, and quartets. Invite some guest musicians to have a part. Feature songs by Fanny Crosby one night, another night songs by Charles Wesley, and another night by someone else. Other possible topics for an evening hymn sing could be, "Hymns of Devotion to Christ," "Hymns of Service to Mankind," "Hymns of the Missionary Spirit," etc. Set aside a portion of the evening time to favorite songs. Let people call out any hymn they wish to sing.

Summary of Suggestions for the Choir Director

1. When scheduling music, consult the pastor and the church calendar.

2. Use discretion and tact when auditioning new choir members.

3. Develop a definite system for rehearsals.

4. Use choir folders to save time and emphasize continuity.

5. Plan music for special occasions; look into opportunities for presenting your music in other churches or hosting a guest choir.

6. Send an invitation to each choir member at the resumption of the choir year.

7. Practice processionals.

8. Place amplification equipment strategically.

9. Plan an evening hymn sing for the whole church.

4
The Responsibilities of the Choir Member

There are many good reasons for singing in a church choir. Singing in a choir is an expression and development of talent. Singing with a good choir can be a pleasant social experience. It is a hobby and even a therapy. It is a good way to get acquainted and to feel needed, wanted, and loved. The choir is a fellowship group of the church; it is a worship cluster in which people feel what they sing and express faith through what they sing. The choir provides a worship art that the congregation may have neither time nor talent to provide for itself. The choir develops leadership and self-confidence in its members and leadership in the congregation in its hymn singing.

These are legitimate reasons for singing in the choir. However, these should be consciously subordinated to a preeminent purpose—*to glorify God*. Most church music expresses praise to God, our aspirations toward God, our need for salvation, cleansing, and forgiveness of sins. It extols Christian virtue, Christian character, and Christian faith. Its words remind us of the importance of prayer, worship, and the Word of God. The subject matter of choir music is holy and devout. It deserves to be sung with feeling and with meaning.

Prayer and the Choir

Prayer is a vital part of the group experience. Prayer before choir is not a routine matter nor a mere technique. Prior to rehearsal, the director can invite his or her choir to share prayer requests, give thanks for recent joys, or petition help for the sick and troubled. The choir members can pray for their director, their organist, for one another, and for continual awareness that the song is to the glory of God. This helps to keep a right spirit and a God-centered consciousness in activity.

Right Attitude—Right Motives

Because we are human we will feel petty rivalries, petty jealousies, and petty resentments over something which is done or which someone has failed to do. We may feel unduly abject over our blunders or unduly puffed up over recognition we receive and successes we achieve. Someone may be given prominent solo parts, while we are given a small part or no special part at all. The director may favor a few and be indifferent to others. We may not like the songs the director selects, and so on. A choir trying to function with rampant negative feelings will be like an engine trying to run without oil in its bearings. Friction in a choir will surely dampen the joy of singing.

Of course the director is only human, like the rest of us, and we have no right to expect superhuman intelligence or angelic virtue in the director any more than we can expect it of ourselves. However, using our imaginations at times may prove useful. Imagine the director of your choir is *Christ*. Think how anxious and eager you would be to follow his direction and sing in a way that would please him. Suppose you knew that he had insight into some of your feelings, and that he could discern when you were puffed up over your excellent performance of a solo. Suppose you knew that he could discern the rankling jealousy or envy you feel inside or the resentment you harbor toward a brother or a sister. If Christ were our director, we would pray to be purged of unworthy feelings, and we would strive to express his praise with sincere motives. Try this exercise in imagination during the opening prayer periods of your choir.

Practice Courtesy

There is a genuine opportunity to practice Christian faith in choir. In fact, unless Christ is foremost in each life, choir may become just an "ego trip" or a hobby. A member of a choir has a real responsibility to other choir members and to the director. These associates believe in what they are doing, and their time matters to them. No one should squander another person's time or trifle with the music that is being sung to the glory of God.

To be specific, here is what I mean by courtesy:

1. Choir members should not straggle in late to rehearsal or to preworship robing time. So many rehearsals get a late start because of latecomers. The morale of the choir suffers because the prompt ones begin to ask themselves, "Why should we exert an effort to be here on time just to sit and wait for the latecomers?" A late start means either a late dismissal of weary people or a premature dismissal, with insufficient time to rehearse. Circumstances sometimes make promptness impossible, but insofar as an individual has control, he or she should always be prompt!

2. Choir members should not carry on a crosscurrent of

talking or whispering while the director is talking. A choir member will never realize what an energy-demanding, emotionally exhausting experience it is to direct a choir unless he or she is a director. The director needs attention to explain meanings of musical terms, to tell what kind of tempo or what sort of expression is desired, and to call attention to errors made the last time a section was sung. While the director is explaining these things, for choir members to be carrying on their own conversation with callous indifference to the director is distressing and rude. Even if the director's instructions are not directed at the entire choir and do not pertain to everyone, the choir can make it easier for the director to talk without having to battle against a buzz in the background. Imagine the weariness and frustration of a director who has explained at length how the music should be sung, only to have certain people "butcher" the music because they carried on their own conversation during the instructions!

3. Choir members should watch the director while he or she conducts. Those who know little about reading music can be guided by the director's cues. This is very important. A choir that keeps together is superior in harmony, and the words of the song are much more understandable. A choir which does not watch its director is like a herd of wild horses yoked together to pull a wagon. Not only will looking up improve the music quality, but also the sound will be amplified. A choir of even a few voices will sound like a large choir if the members look up and project their voices forward as they sing. Life is also a little more pleasant for the director, and his or her work is more rewarding when the director realizes that the choir is really trying to cooperate. With a good director and good

rehearsals, the volunteer choir can gain confidence to sing with less dependence upon the printed music. The result will be gratifying.

4. A choir should support the director in his or her choice of music. It is entirely possible for a wide range of differences to exist in musical taste between a director and some of the choir members. Here again, as in congregational singing, Christian love and tolerance can bridge the gaps. Remember that the director is probably trying to provide music suitable for the text or the theme of that coming Sunday. This narrows the choice. Remember also that some pieces which have irregular tempo or close harmony may produce hideous sounds in the early stages of rehearsal, but after the song is mastered the effect may be beautiful.

Choir members who lack patience, or who don't appreciate the difficulty of the task of choosing appropriate music, may grumble over the music they sing, or sing it with sulky, halfhearted effort. A Christian spirit can tackle even difficult music and produce melody unto the praise of God.

If there exists an unbridgeable gap between choir and director over the kind of music being chosen, the problem should be brought to the pastor and the music committee for thoughtful, prayerful discussion.

Applause During Worship?

Should the choir expect regular applause response to their singing of any number during worship? Should there be applause for solos or individual performances? If a choir is truly singing for Christ, does it need applause as a reward?

Christian musical performances in big evangelistic rallies such as Billy Graham crusades are regularly rewarded with applause. This practice of applause has also become rather common in many churches; so much so that even my questioning of this practice will probably meet with a defensive reaction. Those who defend the legitimacy of applause will probably argue that we live in a new day of worship practice. They will argue that worship was for too long too stiff, too stilted, and too bound by rigid inhibitions. They might quote exhortations from the Psalms to shout, leap, clap the hands, etc. in the praise of Jehovah.

Obviously, there is room for disagreement on this subject. I can only raise the question and express my own serious misgivings concerning applause to reward Christian performance whose prime intent is to give glory to God. To many people, applause shatters the worship effect of a musical rendition in church. Applause may be suitable in a large "rally" atmosphere, but is it appropriate Sunday after Sunday in the local church worship hour? The knowledge that one has earnestly prepared to do the best one is able, and does it primarily to the glory of God, should be accepted as reward enough for the performer or performers.

Systematically Filing and Storing Music

To store the music properly, there needs to be (1) a *place* to store it, (2) a *person* responsible for filing and storing, and (3) a *system* for filing and storing.

The Place

The logical place for filing choir music is in a filing cabinet in the choir robing room. Your church should have a piano in that room so that there can be a brief warm-up on the music before entering the sanctuary. The traditional order of church services is 9:30 or 9:45 A.M. church school and 11:00 A.M. worship. Time between these two services is really very scarce, so every moment counts. It is an efficient use of time to robe, hand out music, and "warm up" in the same locale.

If there is not room for filing cabinets in the choir room, music can, of course, be laid out for each Sunday morning where the choir meets, but it should not be left on the piano or on a shelf Sunday after Sunday.

The Person

Music is expensive. The choir can ill afford to mislay any of its music. If carelessness in music handling is chronic, then it will be necessary to over-order every time to keep the choir supplied; but this is poor stewardship. If music is lost, it is not always possible to replace it when needed by reordering.

Good music deserves more than one rendition. It may be months or even years before that particular piece is sung again, but when the director is ready to repeat the song, he or she would like *every* choir member to have his or her own music from which to sing. People with bifocals or trifocals find it extremely difficult to look on with another choir member. So, I repeat, if the music is filed for future use, *all* the music should be saved, not just part of it.

This focuses our attention on the need for a responsible person to be choir librarian. This person can be elected by the choir or appointed by the director. Even the best system will not work unless there is a person to work it. The librarian can be responsible for handing out music and keeping a record of who has and who has not received the music. If music is to be collected and filed, the librarian can check off the name of persons returning music and those who have not.

There is considerable loss of good music because choir members take the music home and forget to return it. It becomes buried under other papers and for all practical purposes is permanently lost. Some music is carried around the church and mislaid or forgotten in a classroom or left on a shelf. This "shrinkage" of music can be virtually eliminated by the choir librarian. A wise librarian can devise a simple ledger system with the name of each choir member on short, horizontal spaces at the left side of the page. The rest of the page, to the right, can be ruled off with vertical lines. At the top of each vertical column is the name of a piece assigned. These music title columns will intersect with the lines on which are choir members' names. When a member receives his or her music, a check is made in the appropriate column in the space to the right of that name. When this member returns music, the check is circled to indicate music returned. The mechanics of this are really not difficult. When the music is handed out there should be as many pieces of music as there are persons. If there is a shortage, pass out the music and then ask, "Now who didn't receive one?" When the music is returned, check to be sure the number of copies returned is the same as the number originally handed out. If not, ask the choir, "Who didn't return (*name of the piece*)?" A little gentle prodding by the choir librarian will probably be successful in securing the return of that particular music before it is lost and forgotten. The librarian also renders valuable assistance by checking over each piece of returned music for wear and tear. It may be necessary to repair a piece of music before returning it.

The System

A good system for filing music will mean economy in terms

of money spent for music and economy of the choir director's time in searching for appropriate music. A filing system should furnish certain information to make music available for reuse: (1) title of the music, (2) date or dates of previous use, and (3) general theme of the music.

Setting Up the System

You will need a *sturdy* four-drawer wood or steel cabinet and two small card files (like recipe boxes) that hold three-by-five cards. One card file can be used for the *titles* and the other card file for the *topics*. The filing should be alphabetical.

The music itself should be filed alphabetically, according to titles, in the big cabinet. Each set of music is kept in its own file folder. (Booklets containing several different pieces of music should be filed under the first piece.) With that music is a sheet on which is written the dates of previous use or, if it is new music, the date of its first use.

I recommend the use of folders with metal or hard plastic supports across the top that hang from a metal frame (see illustration following). In this type of filing system there are parallel metal rails that run along the sides of the file drawer from front to back, which are supported by clamp-on legs. These legs can be moved to accommodate anything from the full length of the rails to a fraction of their length so that the file can be as long as or short as you want it. Each folder hangs by four hooks and slides on the parallel rails of the file. When a file is removed, the other folders don't collapse into the vacant spot that is left. The space is pretty well preserved so that one can restore the file when finished with it. The metal framework of these hanging files fits neatly into the drawer of a regular file cabinet. The entire unit can be lifted out if so desired.

Illustration of File Folder and File Folders on Rails

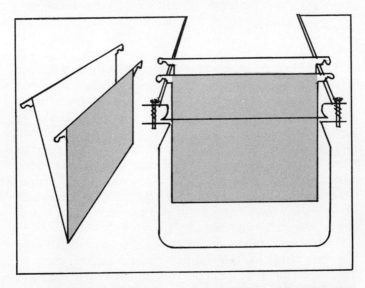

At the top of each folder, there are places for transparent plastic pockets into which one can easily insert a title tab or from which one can remove the tab. For ease in reading, tabs on consecutive folders are usually placed in consecutive positions on the folders—each folder has five possible positions for the title tab (see illustration following). To rearrange the file, one simply changes the location of the folder and the position of the plastic pocket and title tab. The folders are roomy enough to hold a manila folder full of many copies of a particular piece of choir music.

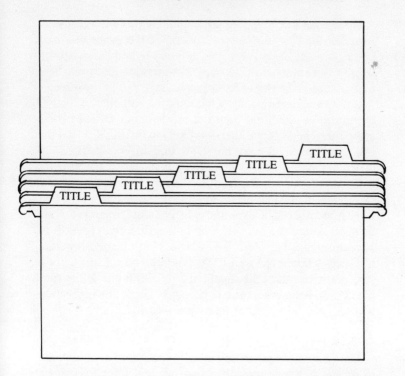

Here is how the system might work. The director is looking for a patriotic number for use the Sunday just preceding the Fourth of July. In his card file of themes under "Patriotic" he finds titles such as these: "Battle Hymn of the Republic," "One Nation Under God," "This Is My Country," etc. If the director wants the music for "This Is My Country," he or she will look in the large file cabinet under *T* where will be found the folder with numerous copies of "This Is My Country," plus a sheet on which are written the dates of its previous use.

Sometimes a search does not so quickly reach a conclusion. Suppose the director cannot remember the exact title of a piece of music he or she wants, but can remember recurrent words in an anthem sung a couple of years ago that would fit in with a sermon the pastor is to preach next month. The director may not even be sure under what topic the anthem was filed. If the music librarian has filed the music under an exhaustive cross-reference system, then it is likely to be found. But if the choir's librarian does not have the time or the experience to do an exhaustive job of cross-referencing, then the director will probably have to flip through the *card file of titles* till he or she comes to one that brings to mind the recurrent words that were remembered. This would consume time, but one can zip through a card file in considerably less time than it takes to paw through a big file full of music. Conceivably there are instances where even a card file would be no substitute for a systematic search of the sheet music file. But one of the card files would help under most conditions. The following section will tell you how to organize your card files.

How to File Music So That You Can Find It Again

Even a single composition usually consists of several pages of music, but for simplicity's sake we will refer to a single composition of music as a "sheet." If your choir always ordered sheet music with only a single title on it, the job of filing it would be most simple. But most choirs buy little booklets which have several titles within them. This is where the card file comes in handy.

Using some mythical titles of choir music, we will show how these could be filed for reference in a card file.

O

"O LORD MOST HOLY" (WORSHIP)
  —"Where God Is Found" (PRAYER)
  —"Seek Ye My Ways" (CHRISTIAN LIFE)
  —"The Joyful Spirit" (CHRISTIAN CHARAC-
                                                    TER)

"O COME, LET US ADORE HIM" (CHRISTMAS)

"ONLY TRUST HIM" (EVANGELISTIC)
  —"Holy Spirit, Faithful Friend" (HOLY SPIRIT)
  —"God Sees the Heart" (CHRISTIAN LIFE)

This, as you see by the tab, is the *O* card in the card file of titles. There is also room on the back of the card for entries. There may have to be more than one *O* card. But the important thing is to take note of how the music is here recorded. In the mythical booklet listed first here, the first piece is "O Lord Most Holy"; so the music is filed under that heading in the big file and also in the title card file. There is, however, also a second card file with subject headings instead of title headings. The *subject* under which the music is filed in the other card file is capitalized in parentheses after the name of the song itself. In that second card file, this song is listed on a card whose title tab reads "WORSHIP." If the director is looking in the subject file for some music to sing on a Sunday when the subject of worship will be featured, he or she would find "O Lord Most Holy" in capital letters. The capital letters tell the director that under that exact title he or she will find the music in the big cabinet file.

Now suppose the director is looking for some music on the Holy Spirit. He or she looks in the card file of topics under the topic card "HOLY SPIRIT" (see illustration following). On the topic card is found the title "Holy Spirit, Faithful Friend," but it is in lowercase letters. That means that this piece of music will *not* be found in the big file under this title heading. But following the title of the music in small letters appears, in parentheses but in *capital letters,* the title "ONLY TRUST HIM." This is the director's clue that the music desired is one of several numbers in a booklet and that it can be found by looking in the big file under the tab heading "ONLY TRUST HIM."

```
                ┌─────────────────┐
                │  HOLY SPIRIT    │
    ┌───────────┴─────────────────┴──────────────────┐
    │                                                 │
    │  "HOLY SPIRIT, COMFORTER"                       │
    │                                                 │
    │  "Holy Spirit, Faithful Friend" ("ONLY TRUST HIM") │
    │                                                 │
    │  "The Comforter Has Come" ("RISE AND SHINE")    │
    │                                                 │
    │  "NEVER FORSAKEN"                               │
    │                                                 │
    └─────────────────────────────────────────────────┘
```

Remember, this card is from the *topic file,* one of the two card-file systems. The topic file is useful when the director wants a suitable piece of music for a given topic but doesn't know what music he or she has available until after consulting with the topical card file. The first title on the above card is in capital letters. The director can find that in the big file under that exact title. The second and third titles are in small letters. They *cannot* (as I pointed out) be found in the big file under their own titles. They *can* be found under the titles which follow in capital letters. This always means that the title in small letters is in a booklet whose first song is the title in capital letters.

Review of Music Filing Procedure

1. If there is more than one song in the sheet music, file it in the big cabinet under the title of the first song.

2. Enter that same title in card file 1 (the title file). Enter it in CAPITAL LETTERS.

    a. Under that title, *indented* several spaces and in *small letters,* write the titles of other songs in that booklet or sheet music.

    b. After every song title (in parentheses and CAPITAL LETTERS) write a topical heading corresponding to the filing of that song in card file 2 (the topical file).

3. Enter every song in card file 2 under its topical heading. After every title which appears in small letters, remember to add (in parentheses) the title in CAPITAL LETTERS with which that song is linked and under which it can be found in the big cabinet file.

4. When an anthem has been performed at worship, return the music to its place in the big cabinet file, and mark on the sheet in the folder the date the music was performed.

Miscellaneous Suggestions

Safekeeping for purses—Most women in the choir prefer

not to take their purses in with them as they enter the choir loft. A large purse is difficult to carry in addition to a hymnbook and a folder of music. The appearance of a choir is somewhat marred by the sight of purses flopping along beside choir members in processional or even normal entry. But the alternative—leaving the purse behind in the choir robing room—can be a risky one, unless there is a lock on the choir's robing room door. We take it for granted that everyone in the church is honest, and this may well be the case. But sadly enough, there are unscrupulous persons who prey upon the trusting nature of the Christian and who prowl through the church building while the church is at worship. Even an experienced usher cannot know every visitor or police every room.

If purses are being left in a choir room, that room should have a good lock on the door and someone in charge of locking that door after the last choir member has departed. Sometimes women in the choir leave their purses with a member of the family for safekeeping. A safely kept purse may not guarantee better singing, but it may prevent a sad aftermath to the worship service.

Social occasions—There is an "esprit de corps" in a happy choir that is further developed and fulfilled by an evening of social enjoyment. Choir members and their spouses can join for a potluck dinner at a home or perhaps reserve a room at a restaurant for dinner. Choir members who are not part of any other church organization need to be included in the social life as well as the service life of the choir. Even those who have social life through other small group activities will enjoy an occasional choir social. The social helps make the choir spirit more cohesive and more congenial.

Summary of Suggestions for Choir Members

1. Examine your attitudes and motives periodically to avoid jealousy or rivalry.

2. Be courteous as a choir member: be on time, be attentive, watch the director, and support the director's choice of music despite your personal preferences.

3. Choose a choir member who will implement and maintain a system for filing music.

5
Youth and Children's Choirs

The benefits of youth and children's choirs are numerous and obvious. There are difficulties too; but the advantages outweigh the difficulties, and it is worth a valiant effort to get one or more youth choirs functioning and performing.

One of the major benefits of these choirs is evangelism. Since children and youth are joiners by nature, and since junior highs and senior highs want to belong to a peer group, the choirs provide an excellent opportunity to engage them in the church. They will hear the preaching of the Word and hear the claims of Christ upon their lives. They will hear, and feel, the pull of the Holy Spirit to become Christians if they are not already Christians. They will be encouraged to make Christian decisions at this most critical time in their lives and will be reinforced in Christian character through worship. Also important in evangelistic impact is the contact nonchurch parents have with the church through their children. The parents may come just to hear their children sing and be attracted to return again and again.

Youth and children are not easily motivated just to come and sit, but they are attracted to the church when they feel they can make a valuable contribution. Choirs for them help hold their interest in church affairs, and feelings of loyalty and responsibility are developed in them that last into adulthood.

Another benefit of these choirs is the cultivation of appreciation for Christian music. Much of the secular music beamed at youth today expresses blatantly anti-Christian sentiments or condones a morality which is not in accordance with biblical standards. Youth who sing in a church choir will naturally develop more discernment and become a degree more critical of the music of the world. Their appetite for good music will increase.

Not by any means least of the benefits is the training of youth for future service as an adult in a church choir. It is surprising how many adults are timid about singing in a church choir because they haven't previously sung in any choir. Even if youth choir members marry and move to another town, one feels satisfaction in the thought that they have become good prospects for a church choir where they will live.

It is no mere coincidence that growing churches have youth choirs and children's choirs. Young adults with children are looking for a church with an active youth program. In their search for a church they are almost as concerned with what the church offers for children and youth as they are with what is offered for adults. A church with good youth choirs and/or children's choirs makes a very favorable impression on young families visiting for the first time!

Getting Started: Step One

The *first step* in getting started is a survey of potential recruits for a youth or children's choir. Study the attendance rolls of church school, youth fellowship, and church membership for potential children's and youth choir members. Make a special effort to discover and include some of the recently inactive persons. This survey will reveal whether it is possible to think in terms of one choir or several choirs and which concentration of ages justifies the effort to begin.

Getting Started: Step Two

The *second step* in preparing for a youth choir is to provide for funding in the budget. This is the responsibility of the music committee in cooperation with the pastor (and a director of Christian education and a youth pastor if the church has these on its staff). If a new job with a salary is being created, the music committee will need to go before the finance committee, and a proposal will need to be made to the church council or the church membership to fund the youth music program through the church budget. There may very possibly be questions raised when such a substantial item appears for the first time in a budget. "Why are we budgeting for a youth choir when we don't even have one?" "Where will we get a director for a children's choir? (or a youth choir?)" The music committee may have to explain that a very fine opportunity exists, along with a very real need, for a children's and/or youth choir and that such choirs can be a valuable factor in the growth pattern of the church and its contribution to the growth and life of the younger ones in the church fellowship. The point should be made that the bargaining power of the music committee should be strengthened by providing funds to pay a director (or directors).

Getting Started: Step Three

The *third step* is to arrange a meeting with the age group for whom you hope to have a choir. It might be helpful to have the pastor, a member of the music committee, and an adult who teaches or works with that age group present during at least the early part of the presentation. The children/youth should sense that the proposed choir is a matter of considerable importance and significance. This is a rather crucial meeting, especially with youth of senior high age. The youth need to be genuinely interested in a choir. They should not feel they are being coerced by adult pressure. One of the adults should be the spokesperson, and the others could be prepared to make a short statement of the value—and the *fun*—of a youth choir. But the adult presence needs to be subdued, and the reaction of the youth should be allowed to be genuine. Very likely the response will be enthusiastic, and your adult initiators will be ready for the next step.

Recruitment for choirs for the younger ages might not be quite as delicate a procedure. Recruitment for a primary choir is about as simple as having the teacher inquire during the church school hour, "How many of you children would like to sing in a primary church choir?" The response might well be almost immediate and unanimous. One would need to get the names of the children present and then contact the mothers for their permission and support to let the children sing in the primary choir.

Recruitment for a junior choir (grades 4, 5, and 6) would be almost as simple as for primary choir. Junior highs (grades 7, 8, and 9) might be a little more wary and a little more doubtful, since boys of that age are beginning to have voice change and may be quite self-conscious.

The survey described earlier will reveal how many eligible voices there are for formation of choirs. The survey might reveal the need for merging primaries and juniors into one choir and junior highs and senior highs into another choir. Or the music committee might deem it wise *not* to merge these different age groupings, but to limit them to—let us say—a strictly junior age choir and a strictly senior high age choir. Such decisions are left to the wisdom of each local church.

Getting Started: Step Four

The *fourth step* is extremely important: selecting and securing a director for each choir. The adult choir director can direct one of the other choirs, and in some churches he or she probably does. Two factors are important here. The first is the director's suitability for leadership of that second choir. Suitability should be considered by the music committee before inquiring about the second factor—the director's willingness to accept a second choir. A director with good rapport with his or her choir is especially important for a teenage choir. In fact, a director skilled in juvenile diplomacy with mediocre music talent would probably succeed more readily with a youth choir than someone skilled in music but blundering with youth.

Perhaps the person who directs choir for the public high school or junior high school would be willing to accept the job of directing a church youth choir, either as an act of service or for an appropriate wage. Perhaps some person with hidden talent in the church will apply for the job. Choosing may very well be a matter of trial and error. One should not automatically rule out musicians with no prior record of youth leadership experience. Some adults have an intuitive knack for rapport with teenagers. Yet I do not mean to create an impossible image of "the perfect leader," for this would discourage the music committee in its search. A director might not qualify for the "Jolly Buddy" award from teenagers but might still be respected and followed as a music leader.

There are really *three qualities* the music committee should look for in its search for directors for these choirs: (1) rapport, (2) musical ability, and (3) Christian life example.

Ideally, every church officer should be a good example of the Christian life. But this is especially true of the person in a position of youth leadership. Teenage youth tend to make idols and models of what they admire. A popular director with low Christian standards could undermine the purpose of a children's or youth choir. Judgment of anyone's character is a rather dangerous practice; so when the character of a prospective director is being considered, it should be done cautiously. During the committee's consideration of a candidate's eligibility, the focus should be on the affirmative qualities of the person rather than the negative.

A spiritual leader of youth will inject more into the choir than just the mechanics or the techniques of singing. He or she will invite the attention of the choir members to the significance of the words they are singing and share what this means to himself or herself in daily experience. The director will encourage the choir to live the Christian life as well as sing it. To some degree, this is also true of the one who directs children's choirs. The youth and children's choir directors become valuable allies of the pastor, the church school teacher, and the youth counselor in the Christian development of the children and youth.

Getting Started: Step Five

The *fifth step* in getting started is to choose an adult assistant to the director. This assistant will be useful whether the choir is a children's or a youth choir. For the children's choir, this adult could be appointed by the music committee. For the youth choir, the adult could be either appointed by the committee or elected by the youth and could be a parent of one of the choir members. Especially for a teenage choir, however, wisdom should be used in choosing this person, for some parents create a "policeman" image that could cause tension. The adult assistant can represent the choir in reporting to the music committee. He or she could provide liaison with other parents where help is needed with transportation, socials, robes, or other matters.

Before the adult assistant begins work, the music committee should give him or her both written and oral guidance in the performance of his or her duties. The youth choir needs to know why an adult assistant is chosen and what is expected of that person. These duties could be listed as: (1) transportation to and from choir for those who need it; (2) filing, distributing, and collecting copies of music; (3) taking roll of attendance; (4) reminding absentees of next rehearsal; (5) reporting to music committee; and (6) communication with parents when a home is needed for a social, transportation is needed for a choir trip, or help is needed for the choir in any other matter. The adult assistant could render useful service to the youth choir by singing with them at rehearsal (*if* that adult has a fairly good voice). Many volunteer choir people learn their music by leaning on the support of a good voice next to them. However, the adult should conscientiously abstain from singing with the youth choir when the members perform on Sunday, unless the youth beg the adult, with a rather united voice, to become a permanent part of the choir. Here is where good sense and intuition must make the decision. It would be better to abstain from singing on Sunday morning than to create any undercurrent of resentment.

The adult assistant will discover that some parents have a dreadful indifference toward their youth's participation in church activities. An appeal to such parents for support may possibly be met with a shrug and a comment to the effect, "I don't tell my son what he has to do. He has to make up his own mind!" If youth feel inwardly rewarded by the joy of singing, their motivation for attendance will be maintained most of the time. However, adult encouragement is always needed.

Special Responsibilities

Be mindful of the fact that many children's and youth choir needs parallel those of the adult choir, such as the filing of music and the care of robes. The adult assistant should be in charge of setting up the filing system. It would be wise for the person who set up the system for the adult choir to explain the system to the adult assistants of the children's and youth choirs. There should be distinctly separate sets of music for each choir and, preferably, separate cabinets, although clearly marked and labeled drawers in one cabinet could serve all children's and youth choirs in the early stages of their accumulation of music. Certainly the children's and youth choirs could have their own card files from the very beginning. If the youth choir wants to borrow music from the adult choir file, this could be arranged with the consent of the adult choir director.

The adult assistant of the youth choir might want to train one of the youth to distribute, record, and file the music. Teenagers are capable of doing this. However, the adult assistant will have to keep a discreet check on whether the music is being cared for efficiently and faithfully.

Little robes for a children's choir are much less expensive than adult choir robes, although they are not necessary to form a children's choir. Youth often prefer some form of distinctive clothing in preference to robes. Boys can have uniform shirts and pants; girls can wear uniform blouses and skirts. This type of clothing creates a feeling of group identity and gives a neat appearance. When an adult choir buys new robes, it may save the old ones. Within a year or two, these discards might lose the stigma of "hand-me-downs" and be acceptable to a youth choir which wants robes. If robes are used, they benefit by some occasional loving attention by mothers of the youth choir members.

The youth and children's choir assistants need to coordinate the social activities of the choirs they work with with the calendar of other children's and youth activities. Choirs should not become rivals of other activities, detracting from them rather than complementing them.

Youth Choir Tours

Many churches which have fairly good youth choirs take their youth on short tours for concerts. This provides incentive for conscientious rehearsals and provides a little tingle of anticipation that converts the work into fun.

Such a tour could probably best be arranged by the pastor, with the help of the youth choir's adult assistant. If a tour cannot be worked out, concerts for one night to neighboring churches probably can be arranged. Parents should accompany these short trips and provide transportation unless the church owns a bus and prefers to take it. These youth concerts are very popular. They convey a message and inspire youth who have no choir in their home church to form a choir.

Everything previously written concerning adult choir guest cantatas applies also to this. Preparation for guest performances stimulates rehearsals and enhances youth pride in what they are doing.

Unique Features of the Younger Age Choirs

Obviously, one cannot make blanket statements that apply equally and accurately to the function and formation of choirs of various age levels. There are differences, and in the foregoing suggestions I have tried to point out some of these differences. I will discuss this subject with a little more detail below.

Primary Choir

Some primary children (grades 1, 2, and 3) are able to read; some are not. The leader can best focus the attention of the children on his or her leadership by having the words printed out on a large sheet of poster paper, poster cardboard, or chalkboard. The choir can be directed to keep tempo with the music by a combination of hand signals and pointing to the words.

Whenever the director of a children's choir discovers that a tape or record is available for purchase with the printed music, he or she would be wise to buy it. Tapes and records are useful teaching tools which can save the director considerable energy, especially if he or she lacks experience and training in music. The tape or record is ordinarily a supplementary teaching tool, and only on special occasions is it a substitute for live piano accompaniment.

Rehearsal times for primary choirs need to be scheduled to allow for early bedtimes, and transportation by parents or older siblings must be arranged.

Junior Choir

Juniors are grades 4, 5, and 6. Some churches provide little organized activity for this age group, so a choir just for *them* is an exciting attraction. Juniors are often sincere, loving, and responsive. The director of a junior choir need not be as well trained in music as an adult or youth choir director, but he or she should be careful to secure music suitable for the junior level.

One need not accommodate to the junior level by confining the music to childish choruses. There are junior hymnals that embrace some of the best in church music but that are simplified to fit a junior's comprehension and ability. It is rather important to create a taste for good music in children and youth. Catchy tunes can be mixed in with their repertoire, but such tunes should not dominate their performance.

It is best to remember that the lower one drops in the age range, the more adult supervision is required for the choir. This applies to distribution and filing of music, transportation to and from home, choir parties planned and supervised with adult help, and adult supervision of robes.

Several cantatas have been written for junior choirs, such as the one about Noah entitled *100 Percent Chance of Rain.* Such compositions usually have some stage construction as a focus for musical activity. They are light, somewhat humorous, and yet capable of teaching truth and Bible story. If there is difficulty securing a capable accompanist, cassette tape accompaniment could be an alternative to live accompaniment. For rehearsals, however, an alert "technician" would be required to stop and start the tape at the director's behest and to rewind and replay with some degree of skill. Such a production is a first-rate means of stimulating the junior's interest in the choir. Neighboring churches usually jump at the chance to invite your junior choir for a special performance.

The Junior High Choir

Junior high choir is similar to senior high, but with some significant differences. Junior highs do not drive, so rather careful provision needs to be made to be sure someone brings them to church and takes them home again.

Junior high male voices have not stabilized, so they need to be guarded against embarrassment during the period of voice change. An experienced director of junior highs will know what he or she can do with the voices in the choir.

Junior highs might not be able to handle the details of distributing and filing their music. The adult counselor for junior highs will have responsibility for scheduling transportation and for filing and distributing music. As with senior highs, an occasional social for junior high choir members will be a good, fun time and will help establish the group spirit.

Scheduling the Choirs

A church with only an adult choir might very well wonder when and how it could *use* four more choirs even if it could create them. It isn't realistic to assume that the average small church will have enough funds or sufficient leadership for an adult choir, a senior high choir, a junior high choir, a junior choir, and a primary choir. Therefore, most churches will have little reason to worry over scheduling problems.

Larger churches might very well have five choirs, but by virtue of being larger they may possibly also have two morning worship services and an evening service. If so, the extra services would be excellent opportunities for using the talents of the children's or youth choirs.

If a small church *were* fortunate enough to have four or five choirs, they could use these choirs to good advantage. The children's and youth choirs need not sing every Sunday, but they could be rotated in use so that every Sunday at least one of them would be singing. Then the adult choir would continue to sing every Sunday, but in addition there would be a piece by one of the other choirs. Blessed is the church which can enjoy such variety in its Sunday morning worship!

6
Meeting the Needs
for Music Instruction

In the average church choir there are some members who are laboring against a handicap of ignorance concerning the rudiments of music. Some of these people are frank to admit their ignorance. Others are embarrassed about it and are even loath to ask questions lest they reveal the depth of their ignorance. A basic understanding of music can add much enjoyment to singing and can improve the total choir performance. The director's job can be made easier if choir members understand their music; in addition, the improvement of the choir's performance will increase the pleasure and enrich the worship experience of the members of the congregation as they listen.

The material in this chapter may be read by a person who feels the need to understand the rudiments of music. I believe this can be helpful, because one does not always know where to turn to find a condensed, concise explanation of insignia and symbols found in church music. For extended knowledge, one should search for some kind of textbook on music theory, but the material in this chapter can be used as "The Beginner's Primer."

I suggest another use of this material. The director can use it as a tool for teaching a special class in music fundamentals. The total choir might be painfully bored by a recital of the simple facts set forth here, but those who are uninstructed might be eternally grateful for a short course that would teach them the meaning of the simplest things they should understand. The fact that a director is thoroughly informed in music fundamentals does not necessarily qualify him or her for teaching these things on a simple level. Not every director is a teacher. Perhaps this material can be a guide useful to the director in a teaching program.

The "Primer Class," or whatever you wish to call it, should be set up at some time other than the regular rehearsal time. It could be half an hour before choir, half an hour after choir, or even at some time on a different day than choir rehearsal. That way, those who know music would not be resentful of their time being taken for things they know so well. Furthermore, those who respond to the opportunity for such a class would feel more relaxed about asking questions if trained singers were not present.

Musical Symbols and Insignia

STAFF = 5 horizontal lines, with 4 spaces between

Treble
Clef
Sign on
a Staff

Music for sopranos and altos is written on the treble clef staff. This is where the women look for their notes.

Bass Clef Sign on a Staff

Music for tenors and basses is written on the bass clef staff. This is where the men look for their notes.

The Alphabetical Names of the Notes

The notes have alphabetical names, derived from the line or space on which they are located. In the illustration following, I show the progression of the notes from the low G on the bottom line of the bass clef to the high G on the space above the top line of the treble clef. The progression goes G,A,B,C,D,E,F,G and this formation is repeated three times from the bottom line of the bass clef to the space just above the top line of the treble clef.

From one G to the next G is *eight* notes, which we call an "octave." ("Octave" is the Latin word for "eight.") There are three octaves from low G of the bass clef to high G of the treble clef. (An octave is not only the notes from one G to the next, but also any eight consecutive notes: from one A to the next, from one B to the next, etc.)

On a piano, the notes progress in the exact fashion that you see them pictured in the illustration. There is no artificial separation between the staff of the bass clef and the staff of the treble clef. However, men's voices and women's voices are so distinct, and their sung parts are so distinct, that the printed music *does separate* the two staffs and keeps them distinct.

For the benefit of your understanding, and so that you can visualize the true succession of the notes, the illustration pictures the treble clef just above the bass clef, separated only by one line and two spaces. This gives the *true picture* of how the notes actually are.

The novice may very well question the value of learning the alphabetical name of a note on a certain line or space. We don't sing those alphabetical names; why learn them? However, the answer is really quite simple. Whenever the director wishes to call the attention of choir members to a particular note, it is not only convenient, but also most often absolutely necessary, to have some exact way to identify *which note* the director has in mind. This alphabetical system identifies a particular note so that all eyes can focus on it and receive instruction concerning it. Later on we will define and illustrate the term "measure." When a director says, "On page ten of your music, in the alto section, the second line and the third measure, look at the D"—that particular note is located as exactly as your house is when you give the town, the street, the house number, the state, and the zip code.

Memory Tricks

When I was a boy, my mother used "memory tricks" to help me memorize the names of the lines and the spaces in the treble clef. The spaces are the simplest. Beginning with the bottom space and proceeding upward, they (only the spaces) spell **FACE.** That one little "trick" by itself could help an alto or a soprano learn to name and locate the notes on the treble clef. Below an F is an E, above an F is a G, etc.

There is, however, another trick which helps in remembering the names of the lines in the treble clef. The lines are E, G, B, D, F. These are the first letters for the sentence "**E**very **G**ood **B**oy **D**oes **F**ine."

In the bass clef, the men can use the following memory associations to help them name and locate tenor and bass notes. The spaces are A, C, E, G. This can stand for "**A**ll **C**ows **E**at **G**rass." The lines are G, B, D, F, A—"**G**ood **B**oys **D**o **F**ine **A**lways."

Fortunately, with continued music experience, one does not have to continue to resort to memory tricks. We become acquainted with the location of notes just as we associate our friends with the neighborhood in which they live.

Range of Voices

There is a difference in people as to the range of their voices. A "bass" singer is a man who feels comfortable singing low notes in the male range. A "tenor" singer is a man who is comfortable singing higher notes in the male range. (Sometimes a director will assign some women's voices to reinforce the tenor section. A woman who normally sings alto can often perform capably on tenor notes.) The average bass voice is comfortable in the range that starts with the bottom G of the bass clef and ends with a D eleven notes above that. The average tenor feels comfortable in the range that starts with the first B of the bass clef and ends with F eleven notes above that.

In the female voices, the average alto feels comfortable in the range that starts with the A two lines below the treble clef and ends with the E in the top space of the treble clef. An average soprano feels comfortable singing from the C one line below the treble clef to the G in the space just above the treble clef.

Since few people are actually "average," however, there will be all kinds of variations to the generalizations I have made.

The Note Stem—Your Clue

Sopranos and altos look for their notes in the treble clef. Tenors and basses find their notes in the bass clef. That, of course, narrows the area which one must cover with one's eye. But sometimes the novice is confused as to which note within his or her area he or she is supposed to be singing. There is a very important clue—*the note stem.*

When two notes are attached to the same stem in the treble clef, the upper note is always a soprano note and the lower one is an alto note. In the bass clef, the upper note is always a tenor note and the lower note a bass note (when they are attached to the same stem).

Suppose, however, that an alto note is on a *separate* stem and is written *higher* than the soprano note. How will altos know that is their note? Won't sopranos think it is their note, since ordinarily soprano notes *are* higher than alto notes? The answer, fortunately, is very simple. When an alto note is written by itself, its stem always points *down*. The stem of a soprano note always points *up*. If sopranos and altos remember this, there should never be confusion as to which section sings which note.

The same rule applies to bass and tenor notes when written separately. The notes with a stem pointing *down* are bass notes. Notes with stems pointing *up* are tenor notes.

Suppose there is only *one note* written in the treble staff. Whose note is it to sing? Does it belong to the altos or the sopranos? If the altos have had a rest, or a series of rests, obviously they should not be singing, and obviously the one note would belong to the sopranos. But suppose there is only one note and neither part has a rest: whose note is that one note? The answer is simple. The one note will have *two stems* attached to it. One stem will hang *down,* signifying that *altos* should sing it. The other stem will point *up,* signifying that sopranos should sing it. In other words, that one note is common property of both altos and sopranos. Both should unite in singing it. THE STEM IS THE CLUE.

Two notes attached to a single stem. Sopranos take the top one; altos take the bottom one.

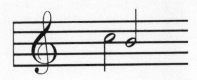

Alto note written above a soprano note. However, altos know their note because the stem points down. Sopranos recognize their note because its stem points up.

One note with two stems attached. Altos and sopranos sing it in unison. Altos recognize their down-pointing stem on the note. Sopranos recognize their upward-pointing stem on the note.

Measure

Remember that a "staff" is five horizontal lines with four spaces between them. The staff is divided in its length by vertical lines called "bars." The spaces between these "bars" are called "measures." They are units of musical time.

Time

Following the clef symbol (whether it be treble clef or bass clef) we usually find two numbers, one above the other. In this illustration we have $\frac{4}{4}$ but you will also find $\frac{3}{4}$ or $\frac{2}{4}$ or $\frac{6}{8}$ or perhaps some other combination. These numbers are important to you.

The top number tells us how many "beats" to a measure. The lower number tells us what kind of note gets one beat. Thus, in this illustration, the numbers give us this information: four (4) beats to a measure and a quarter note (4) gets one beat. The *top* number always tells you how many beats. The *bottom* number always tells you what kind of note gets one beat ("2" = a half note; "4" = a quarter note; "8" = an eighth note; etc.).

Note Value

We need to recognize the basic character of notes in order to assign them a "time" or a "beat" value. (Information on the use of the metronome is found in the appendix of this book. The appendix will be a useful supplement to this material on values of notes and the beating of time.) Here are the notes:

= FULL NOTE

= HALF NOTE

= QUARTER NOTE

= EIGHTH NOTE

= SIXTEENTH NOTE

It is obvious to us from comparison of these notes that the note with a white face and no stem has the most value (that is, will be held the longest time). Adding a stem to the white face cuts the value in half.

Blackening the face of the half note makes it into a quarter note, with half the value of the half note. Adding a "flag" to the stem of the quarter note cuts the value in half again. Adding two flags to the stem makes a sixteenth note, which is half the value of an eighth note.

We can also express this in another way: One full note is equal in value to:

- two half notes
- four quarter notes
- eight eighth notes
- sixteen sixteenth notes.

Once he or she knows these facts, even the novice choir member will realize that when a full note appears it is to be sustained. When a sixteenth note appears, it is to be sung and passed over quickly.

Here is a sample measure (space between two vertical bars). The notes pictured are quarter notes. The time signature $\frac{4}{4}$ tells us that there are four beats to a measure and a quarter note gets one beat. If *one* quarter note gets *one* beat, then *four* quarter notes must receive four *beats*. The above four notes exactly fulfill the prescription of the $\frac{4}{4}$ sign. Five quarter notes would have been too many. Three quarter notes would not have been enough.

Sometimes a song will begin on the fourth beat, so a measure will have only one quarter note in it although the time signature plainly indicates $\frac{4}{4}$ time. This is correct but confusing. The other three beats are added later on in the song. But please ignore this until your director can explain it more completely to you. Ordinarily, each measure should have within it the full number of beats prescribed by the time signature. Obviously, not all notes are quarter notes; so there will be many ways in which a full time count can be given. In $\frac{4}{4}$ time a half note is worth a count of "two beats," so that two half notes in a $\frac{4}{4}$ measure would fulfill the count of four and would satisfy the demand of the signature, as shown below.

One more illustration will suffice to show how the $\frac{4}{4}$ signature can be fulfilled when not all the notes are quarter notes. (In fact, it could be fulfilled if not even one note were a quarter note!)

The first two notes here are eighth notes. It takes two of them to make just one beat. The third note is a quarter note. The signature tells us that a quarter note gets one beat. The fourth note is a half note, which has twice the value of a quarter note, and therefore gets two beats. Adding the combined value of these notes, then, we get exactly four.

DOTTED NOTES—A dotted note has one and one half times as much value as that same note would have with no dot. Let us use an easy illustration. Let us say that this note ♩ is worth two beats. Put a dot after it ♩. and its value is now worth *three* beats (1½ × 2 = 3). A note worth one beat would be increased to one and one-half beats if a dot were placed after it. A note worth four beats would be worth six beats if a dot were placed after it, and so on.

By this time, the novice may be muttering, "Must I be a mathematical wizard to calculate how long to hold every note I sing?" In fact, it isn't that bad. The director, the accompanist, and trained singers have learned almost instinctively how to react to each note they see, so they set the tempo. The novice follows along. However, two things a novice really should do are these: (1) recognize and be able to identify each kind of note and be able to calculate its value, and (2) realize that a dot after a note always means it must be held a little longer than when the note has no dot. It is also important to learn the theory behind music rendition so that with experience will also come increased understanding. With increased understanding one develops more confidence and less dependence upon others for every little thing.

The Director's Motions

Directors use rather standard sets of motions so that if a choir member moved from a church in Seattle to a church in New York, he or she would find the director in New York beating time in the same manner as it was done by the director in Seattle. Below are samples of the patterns of some of these motions:

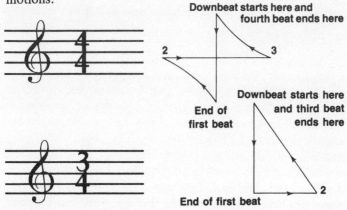

(drawn from director's point of view)

Rests

The word "rest" means just what it says. When we come to a rest, we stop singing for a beat or a fraction of a beat or several beats as indicated by the time value of the rest or rests. When the music shows a rest, the singer should stop singing. When the duration of the rest has expired, the singer resumes singing. One should halt precisely and resume precisely. This gives crispness and clarity to the song.

Full Rest	Half Rest	Quarter Rest	Eighth Rest	Sixteenth Rest

The value of a rest corresponds to the value of a note. For example, a full rest would be worth as much as a full note; a half rest would be worth as much as a half note; etc.

Reading Music

The majority of volunteer choir members profess inability to read music. Perhaps they have a perfectionist concept of what "reading music" means. If it means to pick up a new piece of music and sing through it confidently and correctly for the first time, I would agree that very few people, relatively speaking, can "read music." But actually, anyone who even partially understands and applies music insignia and symbols is reading music. People who have had lessons in voice or piano, school band or orchestra, will have an advantage over those who have had no training. But everyone has to begin somewhere. Most volunteer choir members consciously or subconsciously acquire more skill than they realize in reading music. Through choir experience, they learn to interpret the intervals between notes and translate the change in notes into change of pitch in the voice. In singing new music, each section usually must hear its part played on the piano or organ before being able to sing it correctly. The mind is a marvelous instrument. Almost miraculously, somewhat instinctively, it responds to the challenge of learning by coordinating what the eye reads and what the voice sings.

More Symbols

 —a sharp. This symbol next to a note means, "Raise the pitch of the note one-half tone."

♭   —a flat. This symbol next to a note means, "Lower the pitch of the note one-half tone."

♮   —a natural. It cancels a sharp or a flat that was previously used. It means, "Restore the note to the original pitch it had before being sharped or flatted."

<   —"Crescendo" means, "Increase volume."

>   —"Diminuendo" means, "Decrease volume."

(Notice how truly expressive these last two symbols are. The first sign ["increase volume"] shows two lines opening wider, like a megaphone, to increase the volume of your voice. The "diminuendo" shows two lines narrowing down to a sharp point, shutting down the volume rather than opening up with it.)

⌢   —a pause or hold, sometimes called a "bird's-eye." This gives the director discretion to hold the pause as long as he or she sees fit.

Self-Test

Let the music novice check out his or her sheet or book of music from the church until the next rehearsal and study it carefully to answer these questions:

1. Do I know for sure which notes are mine to sing?
2. Can I give the correct alphabetical name for every note I sing?

3. Do I know for sure how many beats (or what fraction of a beat) each of my notes is supposed to receive?
4. Can I identify every sign and symbol used in the music?
5. Can I give the value of every rest?

I predict that knowledge of the simple facts listed in this chapter will add greatly to everyone's enjoyment of the choir.

Appendix

The Metronome: Aid to Good Music Tempo

Most congregations have struggled with the question of proper tempo for hymn singing. For some reason, it is the natural tendency of a congregation to drag the tempo of a hymn unless there are a forceful songleader and a good accompanist who maintain a brisk tempo. When a hymn is "dragged," it seems to take more breath and more effort to sing it. One becomes weary of the hymn and longs for its conclusion. The effect of the hymn is limp and lifeless, and it seems to lose its power to motivate and inspire.

Recognizing this, songleaders and worship leaders appeal for, and agitate for, more rapid tempo in the hymn singing. Then, alas, the pendulum sometimes swings too far to the other extreme. The congregation is literally raced through a hymn. Unless it is a very well known hymn, the congregation finds the tempo too fast even to read the words, let alone assimilate anything from them. Gasping and stumbling over words, the congregation races to a quick conclusion of the hymn, probably with only the faintest comprehension of the sentiments of the song.

The metronome offers valuable help at this point. Perhaps some musician in the church will lend his or her metronome for temporary use. Perhaps the church might like to own one to have on hand when needed. The metronome offers some objective assistance in the matter of tempo. While it probably would not be used for congregational singing or choir performance on a Sunday morning, it could nevertheless make an impression on accompanist, songleader, choir director, and choir that would be retained in their memories. It would help to guide those who set tempo by impressing on them what correct tempo should be. It could be employed to best advantage sometime during midweek choir rehearsal.

The metronome is a pyramid-shaped object, wound like a clock, with a pendulum that pivots from side to side from the base, with its top free to swing back and forth (see page 108). On the length of the pendulum there is a small weight that grips tightly enough to hold its position but not so tightly that it cannot be moved up or down to a new position. On the face of the metronome, directly behind the pendulum when it is locked into a rest position, there are words and numbers. The numbers descend from 40 at the top to 208 at the bottom. The words (starting from the top and going to the bottom) are: largo, larghetto, adagio, andante, moderato, allegro, and presto. "Largo" is a slow tempo. "Presto" is a rapid tempo. If one raises the weight on the pendulum to the "largo" position, the pendulum will swing back and forth with a maximum slow motion. If one lowers the weight to the "presto" position, the pendulum will swing back and forth with maximum speed. As the pendulum swings, it goes "click, click, click" to sound out the beat or the tempo.

"Moderato" is probably a sort of average tempo that would

be suitable for singing most hymns. However, there is a great difference in hymns. They are distinctive, and their words and their lyrics can best convey their worship thought when sung at the right tempo. Bread has some different ingredients than cake. Salt and pepper are good seasoning for potatoes and gravy but not for ice cream. Hymns, like foods, have their own identity and cannot all be treated alike. It would be a serious mistake to sing every hymn at the same tempo. Not too many hymns should be sung "largo," but neither should many hymns be sung "presto."

Most choir music, and some hymnals, give a clue as to the proper tempo for the song. In some music, just the word for the tempo is given, as for example, "allegro." Some music may also include the number that one finds by "allegro." There may be a "176," which would be meaningful to you if you remember that the range of numbers is from 40 to 208.

Let the director, accompanist, and choir spend one of their sessions singing hymns with the help of the metronome. It would be well for the director to pick out some hymns in advance, choosing a variety of hymns for examples. If the hymnbook does not give any clues as to tempo, the director could do his or her homework and experiment a little before coming to choir. He or she could note in the hymnal, in pencil, what tempo would be suitable, meaningful, and comfortable with each hymn. It is hoped that this choir session with the metronome would help those who set the pace for music to avoid the extremes of either dragging or racing through the hymns in the future.

I have not printed all the numbers which are actually printed on the face of a metronome. I have shown the pendulum so that you can see the words and numbers printed

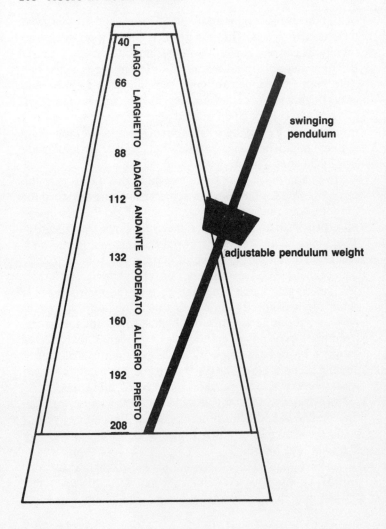

swinging
pendulum

adjustable pendulum weight

40 LARGO

66 LARGHETTO

88 ADAGIO

112 ANDANTE

132 MODERATO

160 ALLEGRO

192 PRESTO

208

on the face of the metronome.

- The tempo of *largo* is between 40 and 60.
- The tempo of *larghetto* is between 60 and 66.
- The tempo of *adagio* is between 66 and 76.
- The tempo of *andante* is between 76 and 108.
- The tempo of *moderato* is between 108 and 120.
- The tempo of *allegro* is between 120 and 168.
- The tempo of *presto* is between 168 and 208.

Important: In adjusting the metronome for tempo, be guided by the above numbers rather than just placing the movable weight near the name of a tempo.

741
3281